A TASTE OF INDIA

SECOND EDITION

Bibiji Inderjit Kaur Khalsa, PhD

Kundalini Research Institute
Training ❦ Publishing ❦ Research ❦ Resources

© 2012 Bibiji Inderjit Kaur Khalsa, PhD

Published by the Kundalini Research Institute
Training • Publishing • Research • Resources

PO Box 1819
Santa Cruz, NM 87532
www.kundaliniresearchinstitute.org
ISBN 978-1-934532-87-4

Project Editor: Sat Purkh Kaur Khalsa
Consulting Editor: Gurumeet Kaur Khalsa
Copy Editor: Michelle Starika Asakawa
Design & Layout: Prana Projects; Ditta Khalsa and Biljana Nedelkovska
Illustrations: Guru Meher Kaur Khalsa. Used with Permission.

The diet, exercise and lifestyle suggestions in this book come from ancient yogic traditions. Nothing in this book should be construed as medical advice. Any recipes mentioned herein may contain potent herbs, botanicals and naturally occurring ingredients which have traditionally been used to support the structure and function of the human body. Always check with your personal physician or licensed health care practitioner before making any significant modification in your diet or lifestyle, to insure that the ingredients or lifestyle changes are appropriate for your personal health condition and consistent with any medication you may be taking. For more information about Kundalini Yoga as taught by Yogi Bhajan® please see www.yogibhajan.org and www.kundaliniresearchinstitute.org.

© 2012 Bibiji Inderjit Kaur Khalsa, PhD. All teachings, yoga sets, techniques, kriyas and meditations courtesy of The Teachings of Yogi Bhajan. Reprinted with permission. Unauthorized duplication is a violation of applicable laws. ALL RIGHTS RESERVED. No part of these Teachings may be reproduced or transmitted in any form by any means, electronic or mechanical, including photocopying and recording, or by any information storage and retrieval system, except as may be expressly permitted in writing by the The Teachings of Yogi Bhajan. To request permission, please write to KRI at PO Box 1819, Santa Cruz, NM 87567 or see www.kundaliniresearchinstitute.org.

This book is dedicated to my beloved husband, Siri Singh Sahib Bhai Sahib Harbhajan Singh Khalsa Yogiji, and my children, Ranbir Singh Bhai, Kulbir Singh Puri, and Kamaljit Kaur, for whom I have always loved to cook the foods they most enjoy.

CONTENTS

Acknowledgments	11
Foreword to the First Edition	13
Food Preparation as a Healing Art	15
Devotion in the Kitchen	20
Serving an Indian Meal	22
Helpful Hints for Food Preparation	24
The Basic Recipes	29
Panir and Chenna	30
Khoa	31
Ghee	32
Ghee	33
Spice Mixture	34
Special Spice Blend	35
Yogurt	36
Snacks and Appetizers	38
Patties and Kabobs	40
Deep-Fried Cashew Patties	40
Deep-Fried Vegetable Rice Patties	42
Corn Patties	44
Coconut Raisin Potato Rolls	46
Crisp Potato Balls	48

A Taste of India
CONTENTS

Pancakes	49
Garbanzo Flour Pancakes	49
Garbanzo Flour Pancakes with Grated Zucchini	50
Garbanzo Flour Pancakes with Mashed Potatoes	51
Garbanzo Flour Pancakes withMung Bean Flour	52
Tofu Jalapeno Pancakes	53
Stuffed Pastry and Biscuits	54
Vegetable Turnovers	54
Deep-Fried Bean-Filled Pancakes	56
Punjabi-Style Bean-Filled Pancakes	58
Party Wafers	60
Deep-Fried Biscuits	61
Punjabi-Style Deep-Fried Biscuits	62
Rich Salted Biscuits	63
Stuffed Pastry and Biscuits	64
Banana with Chat Masala	64
Spicy Cashews and Peanuts	65
Curried Cheese Cubes	66
Story King Janak Plans a Feast	67
# Vegetable Dishes	68
Potato Cream Rolls	70
Onion and Tomato Curry	71
Eggplant Bhartha	72
Stewed Tomatoes	73
Green Chili Stew	73
Chickpea Dahl Curry	74
Leek Bhajia	75
Chickpea-Flour Curry	76
Creamy Spinach and Cheese	78
Ripe Mango Curry	80
Pineapple Curry	81
Yam Curry	82
Royal Potato Curry	84
Kashmiri Steamed Potatoes	86
Dry Potato Curry	87
Potato and Tomato Curry	88
String Beans and Potatoes	89
Green Pea Dishes	90
Mushroom and Pea Curry	90

A Taste of India
CONTENTS

Pea and Potato Curry	92
Carrot and Pea Curry	94
Cabbage and Pea Curry	95
Pea and Cheese Curry	96

Melon and Squash Dishes — 98
- White Squash Curry — 98
- Pumpkin Bhartha: Sweet and Sour — 100
- Bitter Melon with Yogurt — 101
- Bitter Melon and Onions — 102

Vegetable Koftas in Sauce — 104
- Lotus Root Kofta Curry — 104
- Golden Flower Koftas — 106
- Lotus Root Koftas with Mushrooms — 108
- Deep-Fried Panir in Curry Sauce — 110
- Banana Kofta Curry — 112

Stuffed Vegetables — 114
- Stuffed Potato Bhujia — 114
- Stuffed Bell Peppers — 116
- Stuffed Bitter Melon — 117
- Stuffed Cabbage — 118

Tofu Dishes — 120
- Baked Tofu — 121
- BBQ Tofu Ribs — 122
- Curried Tofu with Toasted Nuts — 123
- Chili with Tofu and Beans — 124
- Mixed Vegetables with Tofu Fried Rice — 126
- Pan-Fried Tofu with Nutritional Yeast Flakes — 127
- Scrambled Tofu — 128
- Scrambled Tofu and Peas — 129
- Scrambled Tofu with Green Chilies — 130
- Stuffed Peppers with Tofu and Quinoa — 131
- Swiss Chard Rolls with Tofu — 132
- Tofu Potato Vegetable Casserole — 133
- Tofu Vegetable Stir-Fry with Coconut — 134

Yogurt Dishes, Soups and Salads — 137

Yogurt Dishes—Raita — 138
- Cucumber Yogurt — 138
- Baked Eggplant Yogurt — 139
- Festival Yogurt — 140

A Taste of India
CONTENTS

Banana Yogurt	141
Spiced Potato Yogurt	142
Mint Yogurt	143
Mint Chutney Yogurt	144
Peanut and Raisin Yogurt	145
Crunch Spicy Yogurt	146
Soups and Salads	**147**
Yogurt Salad	147
Curried Cottage Cheese Salad	148
Apple-Vegetable Salad	149
Cream of Almond Soup	150
Story The Holy Man and the Dog	151
Breads	**153**
Successful Indian Bread Making	154
Chapatis	156
Plain Pranthas	158
Stuffed Pranthas	160
Puffed Bread	162
Puris	163
Stuffed Puris	164
Rice Dishes	**167**
Plain Fried Rice	168
Vegetable Rice	169
Mixed Vegetable Rice	170
Sweet Yellow Rice	172
Rice and Mung Beans	173
Split Chickpea and Fruit Rice	174
Coconut Rice	176
Creamy Cheese and Pea Vegetable Rice	177
Royal Sweet Rice	178
Story The Emperor Comes to Dinner	179
Bean Dishes	**181**
Cholay	182
Mung Bean Dahl	184
Black Bean Dahl	185

A Taste of India
CONTENTS

Black Beans with Cream	186
Saucy Chickpeas	188
Kidney Bean Dahl	190

Relishes and Pickles   193

Carrot Chutney	194
Yogurt Chutney	195
Tomato Chutney	196
Sweet Chutney	197
Sweet Fruit Chutney	198
Mango Chutney	199
Spicy Sweet-Sour Mango Chutney	200
Mint Chutney	201
Mint and Coriander Chutney	202
Lemon Chutney	203
Turnip, Carrot and Cauliflower Pickle	204
Stuffed Red Pepper Pickle	205

Beverages   207

Date Milk	208
Milk with Ghee and Almonds	208
Jaljeera	209
Seera with Whole-Wheat Flour	210
Seera with Chickpea Flour	211
Energy Drink	212
Saffron Milk	213
Saffron Milk with Almonds	214
Golden Milk	214
Banana-Almond Protein Drink	215
Fruit Shake	215
Mango Shake	216
Mango Drink	217
Plum Drink	217
Indian Tea	218
Ginger Tea	219
Yogi Tea*	220
Masala Tea	221
Fennel or Oregano Tea	222
Hot or Cold Lemonade	222
Cold, Salted Lemonade	223
Lassi	223

A Taste of India
CONTENTS

Story A Heavenly Dessert	224
Sweets and Desserts	226
Cream Balls and Noodles in Syrup	228
Cheese Balls in Sweet Sauce	228
Cheese Disks in Pistachio Cream Sauce	229
Sweet Cream Balls	230
Gulab Jaman	231
Gulab Jaman—American Style	232
Honey Bits	233
Sweet Noodles	234
Fragrant Sweet Noodles	235
Ice Cream and Syrup	236
Indian Ice Cream	236
Mango Sherbet	237
Puddings	238
Cheese Pudding	238
Royal Pudding	240
Special Occasion Pudding	241
Carrot Pudding	242
Farina Pudding	243
Fragrant Farina Pudding	244
Cookies and Cakes	245
Royal Toast	245
Nutty Cookies	246
Coconut Pastries	247
Fruit Cake	248
Candy	249
Coconut Fudge	249
Pineapple Cake	250
Quick Pistachio-Almond Fudge	252
Almond Fudge	253
Cream Mixed Fruit Bark	254
Coconut Squares	255
Story The Guru's Lesson	256
Special Ingredients and Where to Find Them	258
Index	262
About the Author	264

ACKNOWLEDGMENTS

I would like to thank my sons, Ranbir Singh Bhai and Kulbir Singh Puri, and my daughter, Kamaljit Kaur, for their encouragement and energy that inspired me to write this book and made it possible.

Also, I would like to thank Guru Meher Kaur Khalsa and Gurumeet Kaur Khalsa for their contributions. Thanks also to all of my sisters in divine and beloved friends and family, who helped to kitchen test each recipe.

FOREWORD TO THE FIRST EDITION:
Cooking Is a Key to the Joy of Life

Cooking is an art of life and a science of health. If we love our bodies, minds and selves, we will love to keep them alive and healthy. By eating food which gives us maximum energy we can stand balanced against the outside pressures and the inside traumas.

Wonderful cooking is cooking that can keep us young, energetic and able to face every event in life with perfect self-control and self-posture. Cooking is a key to the joy of a cozy life.

Cooking does not mean just cooking with fire. Cooking means keeping the fire of life going through enjoyment of the warmth, coziness and love of the Beloved, immersed in the dance of Shakti and Shiva.

The science of cooking is the art of happiness—personal, social and communicative. The delight of cooking and its wonderful tastes evoke from within us our best civilized behavior. The enjoyment of cooking brings about the enjoyment of sharing the coziness of life. It is productive and satisfying to the body, mind and soul.

— Yogi Bhajan

FOOD PREPARATION AS A HEALING ART

The traditional Indian healing system, known as Ayurveda, the ancient science of life, teaches that food is medicine. Along with balanced physical exercise such as the practice of yoga, and a positive mental attitude which can be achieved through meditation, the food we eat is one of the three great pillars of total health. Ideally we strive to use locally grown organic ingredients, wherever possible.

A master of Indian food preparation is really a holistic healer. He or she ministers to the needs of the whole person—body, mind and spirit. Simple foods and herbs are the medicinal ingredients. Not only are the ingredients and nutritional values of food of great importance for good health, but so are the color, taste and smell. When her child has the flu, a mother will prepare special stuffed chapatis with onions and herbs to break the fever. A creamy turmeric drink may be served for stiff joints, or a diet of well-cooked beans and rice may be prescribed for digestive weakness. While the ingredients in the dishes are believed to have healing properties in themselves, equally important is the love with which they are prepared and the spirit in which they are served. Through love and service, the Indian cook imparts healing energy to those who partake of a meal.

The traditional Indian diet is purely lacto-vegetarian. No meat, poultry, fish or eggs are included. It is naturally low in fats, cholesterol and uric acid. Simple vegetarian food is referred to in Indian Ayurvedic scriptures as *sattvic bhoj; sattvic* means "pure essence," and *bhoj* means "food." A person who eats sattvic food is likely to be more calm, mentally agile and clear thinking than one who eats heavier foods. The hot spices used in Indian cooking are said to have a "rajasic" quality. This means that they stimulate creative energy, which includes our sexuality and our drive to achieve and excel. Rajasic foods, taken in moderate amounts, are considered to be useful for people who work, or who practice a rigorous discipline such as Kundalini Yoga or martial arts. Through work, exercise and spiritual discipline, sexual energy is transmuted into other forms of creative expression. "Tamasic" foods, such as animal products and alcoholic beverages, are said to dull the mind and lead to sloth and regressive behavior.

A traditional Indian diet includes a balanced amount of protein from wheat, dairy products and rice-bean combinations. Indian medical tradition would say that the Western diet is dangerously high in protein, especially meat centered diets. (The average American consumes about three times as much protein as recommended by the World Health Organization.) Protein, compared to the other food groups, is relatively hard to digest. Too much protein in the diet puts an unnecessary burden on the liver and other organs.

The Indian diet is composed of pure and simple foods—unrefined, unprocessed and natural. While in recent years foreign influences have led to a greater use of canned foods, bleached white flour and refined white sugar, traditional Indian cuisine uses fresh foods, unbleached flour and unrefined sugars. The recipes in this book reflect the more traditional Indian diet. Canned or prepared foods may be used when they do not severely detract from the taste or healthfulness of the dish. Unrefined organic sugar or other natural sweeteners such as honey or agave are used.

As you will see, Indian food preparation relies heavily on several main ingredients. A closer look at them will help to explain why Indian food is so healthful.

RICE. A native crop of India, where it has been grown since the beginning of recorded history, rice is rich in B vitamins and iodine. It is a high-quality protein which is easily digestible and nonfattening. Rice with curried vegetables is very good for the kidneys, for blood purification and for muscle development. I recommend basmati rice, an unpolished white rice from India, or Texmati rice, its North American equivalent. Update for the second edition: Consumer Reports have indicated rising arsenic levels in rice, resulting from soil contamination over hundreds of years. Recent recommendations are to limit rice intake to two and a half servings per week.

QUINOA. Its slightly nutty flavor makes quinoa an excellent alternative to rice. Most quinoa has already been rinsed to remove the saponin, or outer layer, which is not edible. Quinoa has become highly appreciated for its nutritional value, as its protein content is very high (14% by mass). Although not as high as most beans and legumes, quinoa is a source of complete protein, with all of the essential amino acids. It is also a good source of dietary fiber and phosphorus and is high in magnesium and iron. Quinoa is also a source of calcium, and thus is useful for vegans and those who are lactose intolerant. Quinoa is gluten-free and easy to digest. Cooking quinoa is just like cooking rice, for both the cooking cycle and water amounts.

A Taste of India
FOOD PREPARATION AS A HEALING ART

WHEAT. Appropriately named the staff of life, whole wheat is an excellent source of B vitamins and minerals. In the form of bread, of which India has many varieties, it is known as a brain food. When cooked with fruits, nuts, herbs or spices, it can be used for medicinal purposes. The wheat grown in the mineral-rich soil of Punjab, in northern India, is among the most healthful foods in the world.

DAIRY PRODUCTS. Indian cooking uses dairy products that are simple and easy to digest. Yogurt is rich in vitamin B-12, which is essential for the nervous system. Since the body cannot manufacture this vitamin from vegetable sources, yogurt is an important element in vegetarian nutrition. Yogurt neutralizes acidic conditions and enriches intestinal flora. For health purposes, homemade yogurt is preferred over the store-bought kind. Panir is a simple cheese made from whole milk, which has been curdled, drained and compressed. It is lower in fat and easier to digest than cottage cheese or hard cheese. Ghee is clarified butter, that is, butter with all the milk solids and impurities removed. It is the oil of choice in traditional Indian cuisine since it is highly regarded as a nutrient and a preservative. It can be heated to a higher temperature than butter and is lower in cholesterol, yet has a deep, rich taste. Ghee will keep unrefrigerated for weeks.

LEGUMES. The family of legumes, or *dahl* as it is called in India, includes beans, peas and lentils. These foods are useful in enriching the hemoglobin content of the blood. Combined with rice, wheat or corn, they form complete proteins which are easily digestible.

HERBS AND SPICES. It is the unique combinations of herbs and spices that give Indian food its distinctive flavor. Nearly every herb or spice has medicinal properties; however, a few of them are used so frequently that they are worthy of special mention. Onions are known as blood purifiers. They have been prescribed for a long list of ailments including colds, flu, earaches, dizziness and a variety of stomach ailments. Garlic has been called the natural antibiotic. It is used for gastrointestinal disorders, typhus, cholera and bacterial infections. Ginger is soothing and strengthening to the nervous system. It is good for backaches, fatigue, fevers and bronchial coughs, and it stimulates digestion. Turmeric has been recommended as the means of keeping joints flexible and skin and mucous membranes in good order. Recent research indicates that turmeric may be useful in preventing diabetes and cancer. Chilies, green and red, including cayenne and crushed red pepper, are high in vitamins C and A. Despite their hot and pungent taste, they are very soothing to the system. They are good for circulation and digestion and prevent constipation.

A complete list of ingredients and their medicinal properties would fill volumes! Combining ingredients to correct specific conditions is an ancient Indian art. My goal in this book is to offer delicious dishes to balance the whole person in body, mind and spirit. A good experiment for the beginner is to ask yourself how you feel after you've

A Taste of India
FOOD PREPARATION AS A HEALING ART

eaten a well-prepared Indian meal, or better still, how do you feel after you've made Indian vegetarian food an important part of your diet! I hope that your experience with this book will yield very satisfying results.

For more information on the healing properties of food, you can read *Foods for Health and Healing*, by Yogi Bhajan, available from this publisher.

DEVOTION IN THE KITCHEN

Food, family, devotion and community service: The meanings of these words are intertwined in the vast cultural tapestry of India. They are the precious links of a golden chain binding humankind to God and God to creation. A saying in India on the wall of a "langar hall"—the community dining room attached to Sikh temples—reads, "Food and drink are the gifts of God. Service and devotion are contributed by the devotees."

It is with this awareness that we approach the preparation of a meal. It is a privilege to take part in the continuing act of nurturing creation through the art of food preparation. What constitutes a well-balanced meal in India is a mixture of protein and carbohydrates, taste and aroma, beautiful presentation, devotion and love.

On the earthly plane, food provides tangible evidence of the workings of the law of karma, the cycle of cause and effect.

"For what we give, we shall receive. And for every gift that is received, an offering shall be required." God, the giver, provides food to nourish humankind. Human beings, in turn, are obliged to use the strength imparted by food to serve others. Thus, life on earth is an experience in community: the immediate community of family, the surrounding community, and the global community—all mutually serving each other. In this same spirit, over two hundred years after that saying was painted on the wall of the langar hall, Mahatma Gandhi wrote to his disciple, the English woman Mirabhain, "Eat your food thankfully and keep yourself fit for service."

Eating together might be called the "yoga" of family life. For it is in this simple, daily activity that the various members of the family get yoked (yoga) together in a harmonious experience. A meal prepared with love, served in an atmosphere of grace, and eaten with thankfulness brings together the physical and spiritual aspects of life.

A Taste of India
DEVOTION IN THE KITCHEN

The meal is a way to creatively express our love, a time when heart speaks to heart and soul speaks to soul, and we are all nurtured in body, mind and spirit.

It is the undeniable physicality of eating—everyone has to do it to live—that makes food such a wonderful vehicle for building community. In Indian life, among friends and in community gatherings, food is an indispensable part of socializing and an important aspect of any festivity. To offer food to the guest is the duty and pleasure of the host and hostess, and to eat that food to the last morsel is the duty and delight of the guest. Mannu, should read Manu, the ancient Hindu lawgiver, wrote: "Let not the householder eat any food without asking the guest to partake of it; the satisfaction of the guest will assuredly bring the housekeeper wealth, status, long life and a place in heaven." Food given and received in mutual appreciation establishes graceful environments and all other social interactions can be modeled upon it.

Throughout history, eating together has been the most basic form of community activity. It is the great equalizer. The dining table breaks down barriers faster than any bargaining table. When Guru Amar Das was besieged by people wanting his advice, favor or arbitration, he devised a way of setting an atmosphere of peace and harmony among those seeking him out. In an age of prejudice and discrimination, he founded Guruka Langar, or Guru's kitchen—the place where everyone, nobility and peasants alike, had to first sit down side by side, without distinction or discrimination of any kind, and be served a free meal. "First sit in a row in the kitchen, then seek the company of the Guru," he said. Wise politics: a tasty meal tends to enhance a sense of security and well-being and takes care of anxious butterflies in the stomach. It cools the temper and makes one feel already cared for, regardless of the query or complaint. Most important, one glance around the langar hall shows us that everyone—no matter how dissimilar in appearance, how unequal in rank, or how incompatible in emotional or intellectual bias—shares in the human condition that all must eat to live, and everyone enjoys a good meal. The power of food in paving the path of peace should not be underestimated.

Perhaps the best way to bring the nations of the world into harmony would be to spread a dinner table that spans the globe. It would be a wonderful sight, all those different foods, cooked to tempting aromas, being shared in joy and gratitude by all the people of the world—and no reserved seating! Each one of us can start right now, in our own home, by trying the foods of other lands and by sharing the recipes and experiences of the other peoples to forge this eternal link of body and soul—the grace of God through the gift of food.

In our home, it has always been our tradition to serve food to every guest. I would often prepare food for scores of guests on a moment's notice! My husband (Yogi Bhajan) would himself love to prepare a special dish. This was our honor and our privilege to serve healing food to thousands of people who visited.

SERVING AN INDIAN MEAL

An Indian meal is a "mix and match" affair according to your preference. All the foods, except for the appetizers and the desserts, are served at the same time. Vegetable main dishes, bean dishes, rice pilafs, yogurt dishes, salads, relishes, pickles and breads are all present in a magnificent display of color, aroma, texture and taste. Each member of the dinner party gets to choose the order in which his or her food shall be eaten, and "what gets combined with what." You eat a little of samosa along with some hot chutney, then try a taste with a sweet chutney, then a little bit of subji and some raita, then some rice with a saucy vegetable, then a piece of chapati and some dahl ... and on and on in endless variety. Everyone participates in the art of culinary creation within his or her own plate!

At its simplest, an Indian meal consists of a bean dish (dahl), a vegetable dish (subji) and either rice or bread. A normal meal may include all of these, as well as a yogurt dish (raita) and relish. At its most elaborate, an Indian meal will include two or more kinds of dahl, bread, rice, several vegetable dishes and chutneys, a dessert and a beverage. The more festive the occasion, the greater the number of dishes that are likely to be served.

The traditional way to serve an Indian meal is for each person to have a large, steep-sided stainless-steel plate, called a *thali*, on which are arranged several small stainless-steel bowls called *katoori*. Each bowl is filled with a small portion of some vegetable dish, raita or dahl. On the large plate will also be heaped a portion of rice, as well as several different kinds of chutneys and pickles. While the traditional plates and bowls are extremely practical, any comparable arrangement will do. The host or hostess usually spoons all of the courses onto each plate before serving it, and once everyone has been served, checks frequently to see if anyone would like more.

A Taste of India
SERVING AN INDIAN MEAL

A convenient alternative for many Western households is to serve family style or buffet style. Simply spread out all the different dishes in serving bowls and let everyone help themselves.

Appetizers are usually served informally before sitting down to dinner, often while the meal is still being prepared. Drinks such as lassi or fruit juice may be served as well. During the meal, the only liquid served is water. After everyone has eaten to complete satisfaction, the table is cleared and the sweet course brought in, sometimes with hot tea. And somehow, through the miracle of Indian cooking, everyone does manage to eat just a little bit more!

HELPFUL HINTS FOR FOOD PREPARATION

Some of the ingredients in Indian cooking must be specifically prepared before using. They are listed below. I've also shared some helpful hints about cooking and storing various foods.

Almonds can be peeled by putting them into a bowl and covering them with boiling water. After about 10 minutes pour off the water. You can then just "pinch" the skins right off. Or you can soak the almonds in cold water overnight, and by morning they will be ready to peel easily.

Beans have to be very carefully picked over before using. The simplest way to do this is to spread out the beans (or lentils or dried peas) in one layer on a cookie tray and sift through with your fingers and a sharp eye, looking for stones and debris. Very often the stone and bean look deceptively alike. After you've picked out all the stones, place the beans in a bowl, cover with water and swish the beans around. Any remaining dirt or debris will rise to the top of the water. Carefully pour off the water and wash once or twice more, until the water is clear.

Cardamom pods: to take out the little black seeds inside, press the pods with a mortar and pestle. Then discard the pod. If you are de-seeding a lot of cardamom pods, spread them out in one layer on a clean surface and roll over them, pushing hard, with a rolling pin a few times, so you can liberate the seeds.

Chili powder blends can be either mild or hot, according to preference. For hotter blends, add cayenne pepper to the normal mild chili powder blend.

Coconuts should be chosen free from cracks or mold. To open a coconut you can either pound around the "equator" of the coconut with a hammer until the shell cracks open or you can "bake" it open. Just drill two holes in the "eyes" and drain out the milk. Then put the coconut in a 400-degree oven for 15–20 minutes. The shell will shrink. Take it out, hit it with a hammer and the shell should crack open. You can then peel away the brown inner skin with a sharp knife or vegetable peeler. Break into pieces and wash off any debris.

To grate the coconut, cut it into little pieces and toss into an electric blender or food processor (with the metal blade), or hand grate it on the small holes of a metal grater. Extra-fine grated coconut freezes very well (but freeze it in small batches, because once defrosted, it does not freeze well again).

Coriander leaves (cilantro) make a nice addition to any Indian meal. Place finely chopped leaves in a bowl on the table as a do-it-yourself garnish.

Deep-frying requires that the ghee or oil reaches its highest heat without burning, about 375 degrees, just before the smoking point. If it begins to smoke, turn down the heat. To test whether your oil is hot enough, stand back (oil splatters) and throw a sprinkle of water into the oil. It should crackle and pop wildly.

The important thing in deep-frying is the freshness and flavor of the oil. For most deep-fried foods, either ghee or a bland oil such as sunflower or corn oil is best. After you've finished frying the food, let the oil cool down. Most of the debris from cooking will sink to the bottom of the pan. You can then pour off the top oil, straining it through several layers of cheesecloth into a jar, and store it for reuse in the refrigerator. If the oil has taken on the smell of the food you've just fried, you can reuse it for frying strong-tasting foods like onions, garlic and ginger. Don't mix your oils or fry sweet delicate-tasting food in oil that has been used for spicy foods. Deep-frying with ghee is especially delicious, and the same method can be used to recover the leftover ghee. Refrigerate leftover ghee because it is no longer as pure as fresh ghee and can spoil.

Freezing Indian food is very simple. Most dishes with gravy, "dry" vegetable dishes and bean dishes freeze very well. Rice, yogurt and sweet puddings lose their texture in freezing and are therefore not good choices for quantity cooking. In reusing frozen Indian food, the most important thing is to defrost properly. Take the food out of the freezer the night before and let it defrost completely before reheating. This way the texture stays the same and the delicate flavors can re-permeate the vegetables. Then place it in a saucepan and slowly heat it. Herbs and spices lose much of their flavor in freezing, so you might want to perk up the reheated dish with some garam masala.

Most breads freeze well and can be reheated in the oven or toaster oven. Samosas and koftas (vegetable balls) can be reheated by re-deep frying. Gulab Jamans, the sweet balls, can be frozen in plastic bags without having been cooked in their syrup. When needed, let them defrost, then cook them in a honey syrup for a few minutes before serving.

A Taste of India
HELPFUL HINTS FOR FOOD PREPARATION

Garlic should be felt carefully before buying to make sure there are no "empty feeling" spots—this indicates rotting or very old garlic that is shriveled up inside. To peel garlic easily, just break the bulb into cloves and place a clove under the flat side of a large kitchen knife. Press down firmly and smash the clove. The peel will break open and you can remove it easily.

If you've eaten a dish laced with garlic and are concerned about your breath, chew on green cardamom seeds, a clove, or some fennel seeds. Cardamom seeds also aid digestion.

Ginger is very knobby, with odd angles and protuberances. You can easily slice these odd pieces off and use them for making ginger tea, or you can carefully peel or scrape around them with a small sharp knife or a vegetable peeler. When you have a piece of ginger peeled, lay it on a cutting board and slice it very, very thinly with a sharp knife. You will find that each piece of ginger has a "grain," along which it slices easily. Then stack these slices in a pile and slice them again into long, thin, match-stick pieces. Gather these into a bundle and dice them into tiny bits. If not chopped carefully, your ginger may end up as a stringy lump rather than individual pieces.

Green chilies can be hot. They are sold fresh in most ethnic food stores and many supermarkets. They vary in size and length, but the ones traditionally used in Indian cooking are about 2–4 inches long and very thin. If not available, use Mexican jalapeno or serrano chilies (mild green chilies, roasted so that skins can be removed, can be substituted if you prefer). The range of hotness varies considerably, so try a bit of each chili before you use it to determine how much you really want in that recipe. Experienced cooks can tell the hotness just by braking a chili and smelling it, and with a little experience you can, too. The wide stem end of the chili is hotter than the narrow tip, and the core and seeds inside are the hottest parts. For the timid, therefore, it is best to remove the insides, cut off the stem end, slice the chili in half lengthwise and scrape out the core and the seeds.

Just by handling a green chili you may experience a burning sensation on your hands. Use plastic gloves if you have sensitive skin or if you are going to handle a baby afterward. Be sure not to touch your face, especially your eyes, until you've washed your hands thoroughly with soap and water. The burning is caused by an acid in the chili. If necessary, use milk or baking soda to neutralize it.

Pan frying: Start off with the oil warm rather than hot and let the ingredients and the oil then heat up to frying temperature together. This helps assure even frying. Hard spices such as mustard seeds, coriander seeds and fenugreek seeds take longer to fry than softer seeds such as cardamom or cumin, so start them off first. In frying onions, garlic and ginger, first fry the onions until they are almost done—limp, translucent and brown—then add the garlic and ginger, since they take much less time to brown.

A Taste of India
HELPFUL HINTS FOR FOOD PREPARATION

Because nuts contain so much oil, once they've given up their moisture, they tend to burn very quickly, so keep a vigilant eye on the frying pan.

Pressure cooking saves time, improves food flavor and color, preserves vitamins and minerals, and lowers cooking fuel costs. As such it is a worthwhile addition to any serious cook's kitchen. It is particularly useful in Indian cooking as a means of cutting in half the cooking time for bean (dahl) dishes and is also useful in cooking vegetables.

The best kind of pressure cooker is stainless steel, which does not react with foods being cooked. The instruction booklet that comes with your pressure cooker should indicate modifications of cooking time and quantities (such as amount of water to be added) when cooking with the pressure cooker.

Rice, when purchased in bulk food stores, is often full of debris such as bits of vegetable matter, dirt and pebbles. First, stones should be picked carefully, then wash the rice by placing it in a large bowl and running cool water over it. Swish the rice around with your hands. The debris and a whitish powder will rise to the top of the water. Carefully pour off the water and repeat the washing process two or three times, until the water is clear.

Roasting spices, nuts or flour requires even more vigilance than frying. To roast, first heat your thick-bottomed frying pan, then add the spices or nuts, shaking the pan continuously. The spices or nuts are done when they are deep brown but not burnt. Spices can then be ground with a mortar and pestle or in an electric coffee grinder or blender. Store ground spices in an airtight container away from light.

THE BASIC RECIPES

Fragrant and enticing, traditional Indian meals rely upon a few basic recipes: garam masala, ghee, chenna, panir, khoa and yogurt. They form the foundation upon which the temple of Indian cuisine is built. Any one of them may be used in the preparation of several dishes within the same meal. The ghee prepared for stuffed prantha is used in Bengali-Style Potatoes and Cabbage as well as sweet laddu; the cubes of panir are equally delicious soaking up the pistachio cream of rasmalai or swimming in the tangy tomato sauce of Matar Panir. Once these basic recipes become a part of your repertoire, delicious, authentic Indian meals can be easily prepared.

A Taste of India
THE BASIC RECIPES

Panir and Chenna
(SOFT LIGHT CHEESE)

PANIR (paneer) is *the* Indian cheese, similar to Italian ricotta cheese but much drier. Made from split milk, in the rough curd form it is called chenna, and when it is compressed and cut into cubes it is called panir. It is used in many aspects of Indian cookery: appetizers, main dishes and desserts.

½ gallon whole milk
¼ cup lemon juice or 3 teaspoons cream of tartar plus 1 cup hot water

① In a large, thick-bottomed saucepan, heat the milk to the boiling point, stirring frequently to avoid sticking. Remove from heat. Immediately and little by little, add the lemon juice or cream of tartar dissolved in hot water, stirring gently. When the milk splits into lumpy, white curds and a watery, greenish whey, stop adding lemon juice or cream of tartar. Cover and let stand for 15 minutes.

Note: If too much lemon juice or cream of tartar is added, the panir will be suspended in the whey in fine particles, which are very difficult to separate out.

② Line a colander with several layers of cheesecloth. Place the colander in the sink or a large bowl if you intend to keep the whey. Pour the curdled milk into the colander. The cheesecloth will allow the whey to drain through and trap the curds.

③ When all the liquid is drained off, wrap the cheesecloth tightly around the curds and hang this "bag" of curds over the sink or a bowl to let any remaining liquid drip off from the curds. The curds, once they have been drained, are called *chenna*.

A Taste of India
THE BASIC RECIPES

 When no more moisture is dripping off, put the wrapped curds in a baking dish, placing a heavy weight on top of the curds, and then cool in the refrigerator overnight. This will form the curds into a solid mass, called *panir*. In the morning, unwrap the panir and cut into cubes or mold into balls.

Note: Panir will keep fresh in the refrigerator for 3–4 days. If you need to store it for a longer period, panir can be frozen. The whey is a healthy drink. Children love it mixed half-and-half with apple juice.

Khoa
(UNSWEETENED CONDENSED MILK)

KHOA, made from whole milk, is the creamy, fudge-like base of many exquisite Indian candies and sweets. It takes a fairly long time to make—the milk cooks down slowly to about one-quarter of its volume—but it really is the only way to get that incredible light creaminess which makes barfi such a special treat. (If, however, you are very pressed for time, you may substitute canned unsweetened evaporated milk for khoa.)

½ gallon whole milk

In a large, thick-bottomed saucepan, heat the milk to boiling, stirring continuously to prevent sticking. Keep boiling and stirring vigorously until the moisture is evaporated from the milk and a smooth, very thick cream is formed. Remove from the heat and let cool. Store in a covered container in the refrigerator.

Yield: 2-½ cups khoa.

A *Taste of India*
THE BASIC RECIPES

Ghee
(CLARIFIED BUTTER)

GHEE is butter that is allowed to simmer for a long time so the moisture from the milk solids evaporates completely. Meanwhile, the impurities in the butter sink to the bottom of the pan as a discardable residue. Ghee has a wonderful, slightly nutty flavor and is very low in cholesterol.

Note: Ghee keeps without refrigeration for 3–4 months when stored in a closed container, up to 1 year in the refrigerator, and nearly forever frozen. Therefore, since it is time-consuming to make, it pays to make a large quantity at a time. Once you start using ghee instead of oil for frying and in place of butter on toast, you won't want to use anything else. However, if you want to start small, one pound of unsalted butter will yield approximately 1½ cups of ghee.

To make ghee you will need a 12-quart, stainless-steel, thick-bottomed pot. (In the process the ghee foams up, so you will need to leave plenty of room in your pot.)

9 pounds unsalted butter

1 Over low heat, slowly heat the butter until completely melted, then raise the heat to high and continue cooking, stirring often. Take care to frequently scrape the bottom of the pot. The butter will come to a foaming boil, and the heat may need to be reduced until the foam subsides to keep it from boiling over.

2 After about 12–15 minutes of boiling, the butter oil (ghee) will start to show a separation from the milk solids. The oil is translucent yellow, and the milk solids are thick and white. Continue cooking and stirring.

A Taste of India
THE BASIC RECIPES

③ After 5–8 more minutes, the oil will separate out more, becoming almost clear, and the solids will disintegrate into small particles with a slightly reddish-orange tinge, indicating the ghee is done. The smell is delicious. Remove the pot from the stove to a safe place where it will not be disturbed as it cools. When the ghee is properly cooked, all of the milk solids will settle to the bottom of the pot.

④ After several hours, carefully pour off all of the ghee into a clean, wide-mouthed glass gallon jar through several layers of cheesecloth (held onto the jar with rubber bands). Store at room temperature with the jar covered. Discard the milk solids.

Yield: 9–13 cups ghee

Ghee
SLOW-COOKER METHOD

4 pounds unsalted butter

Place the butter in a 6-quart slow cooker. Let cook at medium heat for 12 hours, then... ghee! Just pour off the oil as described in above recipe and store in a glass jar.

Yield: 6 cups of ghee

A Taste of India
THE BASIC RECIPES

Spice Mixture
(GARAM MASALA)

GARAM (warm or hot) masala (blend) is a unique combination of health-giving spices. The terms *warm* and *hot* do not refer to the "spiciness" on the palate, but to the medicinal properties of the spice. Warm or hot spices are those that help generate body heat and are therefore good to eat in cold weather. Bay leaf, black cardamom, cinnamon, ginger, mace, nutmeg and red pepper are examples. Cool spices are those that take heat away from your system: fennel, cloves and green cardamom are some examples of cooling spices.

There are many different blends of garam masala. As you become more familiar with the recipes in this book and sensitive to your own subtle taste preferences, you might find yourself varying these basic garam masala recipes a bit to suit your own needs. Imported garam masala can be purchased in tins or boxes in Indian specialty food stores and even some supermarkets, but they are sometimes stale from long periods of shipping and storage. Since so much of Indian food's special taste, aroma and benefits comes from the spices, it really pays to make your own garam masala.

1 cup coriander seeds

1½ cinnamon sticks (about 4 inches)

½ cup cumin seeds

½ cup black peppercorns

In an electric blender, coffee grinder or spice mill, grind the spices to a fine powder. Store in an airtight container.

½ cup black cardamom pods (use only seeds)

¼ cup whole cloves

1 teaspoon ground nutmeg

Yield: 2 pints

A Taste of India
THE BASIC RECIPES

Special Spice Blend
(GARAM MASALA)

There are as many kinds of masala as there are cooks in India. Here is my "Special Masala," which you may choose for use in some recipes.

1 teaspoon ground black pepper

½ teaspoon salt

1 teaspoon ground cumin

1 teaspoon red chili powder

3 teaspoons mango powder

Mix all the spices together. Store in an airtight container.

Yield: ¼ cup

A Taste of India
THE BASIC RECIPES

Yogurt
(DAHEE)

YOGURT, whether served plain or with vegetables and seasonings, is a part of most Indian meals. Although store-bought yogurt can be used, for real authentic taste and consistency, and for maximum health benefits, homemade yogurt is best. Here's how to make it:

1 quart milk

2–3 tablespoons plain yogurt

Pour milk into saucepan. Heat it slowly so as not to scorch it. Just short of boiling, remove it from the heat and let it cool to a lukewarm temperature, about 118 degrees. As it cools, stir it occasionally. Then add 2 to 3 tablespoons of yogurt as a "starter" and stir gently and thoroughly. You can leave the milk in the saucepan, covering it, or you can pour it into a sterilized jar with a lid. Wrap snugly in a towel to hold in the heat, and place in a warm, dark place where the temperature can be maintained for 6 to 7 hours. A gas oven with only the pilot light on works well. An insulated cooler or a cardboard carton covered with a blanket can also be used. Let it sit undisturbed. The temperature must be neither too hot nor too cold, or the yogurt won't form. After 6 to 7 hours, you can remove it from its "hiding place" and refrigerate.

Yield: 1 quart

SNACKS AND APPETIZERS

Formally, the Indian meal consists of only the main course followed by the sweet course. However, it is quite common for Indian families to serve a beginning course of snacks or appetizers while everyone is waiting for dinner to be served, especially when guests have been invited.

Salty or savory snacks *(chat)* are, for the most part, deep-fried finger foods or rich, filled pastries. When serving these as an opening to a meal, go easy. These foods are very rich and extremely delicious. The tendency to fill up on appetizers can blunt the comfortable enjoyment of the rest of the meal.

A Taste of India
SNACKS AND APPETIZERS

Outside of dinner hours whenever a visitor arrives, snacks are served, usually with hot or cold drinks, depending on the season. It's considered the most basic form of hospitality, deeply rooted in Indian tradition. Since snacks are served so often, and since they must be ready at a moment's notice, the culture of India has developed a great variety of easy-to-make snack items that either store well or can be whipped up fresh at a moment's notice. These are often served with a choice of tangy or sweet chutneys for dipping. When necessary, snacks can serve as a very tasty light meal.

Many of the filled pastries and balls can be made in quantity, frozen and then deep-fried as needed. The biscuits and crackers will keep fresh for a long time when stored in an airtight container.

Snack time in India includes both sweet and salty snacks served right alongside each other. Recipes for the sweet snacks can be found in the chapter on sweets and desserts.

A Taste of India
SNACKS AND APPETIZERS

Patties and Kabobs

❧

Deep-Fried Cashew Patties

For the patties:

1 teaspoon ghee

2 cups fresh bread crumbs

4 teaspoons unbleached white flour

1 cup matzo meal (Manischewitz)

4 green chilies, hot or mild to taste, seeded

1 cup coarsely chopped cashews

1½ cups milk

¼ cup fresh coriander leaves (cilantro)

3 teaspoons tomato sauce

½ teaspoon mustard powder

¼ teaspoon ground white pepper

½ teaspoon salt, or to taste

① In a large, thick-bottomed frying pan or wok, heat the ghee and sauté the 4 teaspoons of unbleached white flour and the green chilies for about 2 minutes, until the flour is slightly browned. Add the milk and cook for 3–5 more minutes, until thickened, stirring continuously. Then add the fresh bread crumbs, cashews and coriander leaves. Continue to cook 2–3 more minutes, stirring continuously, until very thick. Remove from the heat.

② Add the tomato sauce, white pepper, mustard and salt, mixing thoroughly. Spread this mixture onto a cookie tray and press it down flat. Place it in the freezer for 15 minutes, until it becomes firm.

③ In a bowl, mix ½ cup of unbleached white flour with enough water to form a batter (about ½ cup).

④ Remove the cashew spread from the freezer and cut out patties with a heart-shaped cookie cutter. Dip each one in the batter, coat it completely with fine bread crumbs.

⑤ In a thick-bottomed saucepan, heat the vegetable oil or ghee (See "Deep Frying," page 25). Carefully immerse 3–4 patties in the hot oil and deep-fry until golden brown, 2–3

A Taste of India
SNACKS AND APPETIZERS

For the batter:

½ cup unbleached white flour

½ cup fine dry bread crumbs, for dusting

½ cup water

For deep frying:

2 cups vegetable oil or ghee

For the decoration:

A few lettuce leaves

1 radish, sliced thinly

1 tomato, wedged

2 cups oil or ghee for deep-frying

6 minutes. Remove with a slotted spoon, letting the excess oil drip back into the pan. Drain further on paper towels.

6 Serve the patties arranged on a bed of cooked basmati rice and garnish with lettuce, radish and tomato. Serve with mint or tomato chutney for taste.

Yield: 6 patties

Note: Served alone they make a high-protein breakfast food.

A Taste of India
SNACKS AND APPETIZERS

Deep-Fried Vegetable Rice Patties

A crispy main dish with a mild flavor.

For the patties:

2¼ cups milk

3 tablespoons ghee

5 green chilies, mild or hot, to taste, chopped

½ teaspoon salt to taste

½ teaspoon mustard powder

2 small carrots, diced and steamed

1/3 cup green peas, cooked

1/3 cup or more of rice powder

2–3 coriander leaves (cilantro)

1 tablespoon tomato sauce

For the batter:

1 cup unbleached white flour

1 cup water

❶ In a thick-bottomed saucepan, boil the milk with the green chilies and 3 tablespoons of ghee. Stir in the rice powder and cook it, stirring continuously until it becomes quite thick. (Add a little more rice powder, if necessary, to thicken.) Add the carrots and peas. Remove from the heat. Mix in the coriander leaves, salt, mustard and tomato sauce. Stir thoroughly.

❷ Spread this mixture onto a cookie sheet and refrigerate until it is solid. Then remove from the refrigerator and cut into patties with a large cookie cutter.

❸ In a bowl, combine the unbleached white flour and water. Dip the patties into the batter, then into the bread crumbs.

❹ In a thick-bottomed saucepan, heat the 2-3 cups of vegetable oil or ghee for deep frying. Carefully immerse the patties in the oil and fry until golden brown, 2-3 minutes on each side. Remove with a slotted spoon, letting the excess oil drip back into the pan. Drain further on paper towels.

A Taste of India
SNACKS AND APPETIZERS

1 cup fine dry bread crumbs, for dusting

2–3 cups vegetable oil or ghee for deep-frying

For decoration:

1 boiled beet

1 cucumber

1 tomato

2–3 lettuce leaves

5 Serve piping hot, arranged on a platter decorated with sliced colorful vegetables such as beet, tomato, cucumber, and lettuce leaves.

Yield: about 20 patties

A Taste of India

SNACKS AND APPETIZERS

Corn Patties
(MAKEE VADAA)

1 cup maize (dried whole corn kernels)

3 cups hot water

1 medium onion, chopped

1 teaspoon ground black pepper

2 tablespoons lime juice

2 tablespoons chopped green chilies, mild or hot to taste

½ teaspoon salt, or to taste

1 tablespoon unbleached white flour

2 teaspoons cumin seeds

2 cups vegetable oil or ghee for deep-frying

1. Immerse the corn in hot water and let soak overnight.

2. Drain the water off the corn. In a blender, grind the onion, then add lime juice, corn, chilies, cumin, black pepper, salt and flour. Blend until a thick paste is formed.

3. Form paste into small balls each about the size of a walnut, then flatten them out into thick patties.

4. In a thick-bottomed saucepan or wok, heat the vegetable oil or ghee. Immerse the patties in the hot oil and deep-fry until golden brown. Remove with a slotted spoon, letting the excess oil drip back into the pan. Drain further on paper towels. Serve hot.

Yield: 20 patties

A Taste of India
SNACKS AND APPETIZERS

Deep-Fried Farina Patties
(SOOJEE TIKKEE)

For the patties:

1 cup milk

2¼ cups farina

2 tablespoons sweet butter

2 green chilies mild or hot, to taste, chopped

1-½ teaspoons finely chopped fresh coriander leaves (cilantro)

½ teaspoon crushed dry red chilies

1 teaspoon salt, or to taste

½ teaspoon finely chopped peeled fresh ginger

1 ½ teaspoons tomato sauce

For the batter:

½ cup unbleached white flour

½ cup water

½ cup fine dry bread crumbs for dusting

2 cups vegetable oil or ghee for deep-frying

① In a thick-bottomed saucepan heat the milk and butter together, then add the farina. Cook on a low heat, stirring continuously, until the oil starts to separate out. Add the green chilies, crushed red chilies, ginger, coriander leaves, salt and tomato sauce, stirring well.

② Spread the mixture on a cookie sheet and refrigerate until it hardens. Remove from the refrigerator and cut into simple patty shapes with a cookie cutter.

③ In a bowl, make a thin batter of unbleached white flour and water. Carefully dip the patties into this batter and then into the bread crumbs.

④ In a thick-bottomed saucepan, heat the vegetable oil or ghee for deep frying. Carefully immerse the patties in the hot oil and deep-fry until golden brown, about 3–4 minutes. Remove with a slotted spoon, letting the excess oil drip back into the pan. Drain further on paper towels.

Yield: 9–10 patties

A Taste of India
SNACKS AND APPETIZERS

Coconut Raisin Potato Rolls
(AALOO KABAAB)

A delightful and unusual appetizer.

For the kabobs:

2 large potatoes

3 teaspoons salt

2 tablespoons ghee (for stuffing)

1 small tomato, chopped

1 tablespoon raisins

1½ cups grated fresh coconut

1 teaspoon peeled and finely chopped fresh ginger

2 slices toasted or dry bread, crust removed, crumbled

1 tablespoon fresh chopped coriander leaves (cilantro)

1 teaspoon ground white cumin

2 green chilies, mild or hot, to taste, chopped fine

½ teaspoon garam masala

1 Boil the potatoes in water with 2 teaspoons of salt for about 15 minutes. When tender, remove from water, let cool, then peel (if desired) and grate.

2 In a thick-bottomed frying pan or wok, melt the 2 tablespoons of ghee and add the fresh coconut, ginger root, coriander leaves, green chilies, tomato and raisins. Add 1 teaspoon salt, crumbled bread, cumin and garam masala. Mix all together and fry for about 3 minutes. Add the grated potatoes, mix well and set aside.

3 Make a thick batter of the flour and water. Flour your hands, and take a small handful of the potato mixture and form into an oblong roll about 2 inches long. Dip the roll in the batter and coat it with bread crumbs.

A Taste of India
SNACKS AND APPETIZERS

For the batter:

½ cup unbleached white flour

1 cup water

1 cup fine bread crumbs

2 cups vegetable oil or ghee for deep frying

 In a thick-bottomed saucepan, heat the 2 cups of vegetable oil or ghee for deep frying. Carefully immerse the potato rolls in the hot oil and deep-fry until golden brown. Remove with a slotted spoon, letting the excess oil drip back into the pan. Drain further on paper towels. Serve hot with chutney.

Yield: 20–25 kabobs

A Taste of India
SNACKS AND APPETIZERS

Crisp Potato Balls
(ALOO BONDA)

1/3 cup small or instant tapioca

2 cups water

2 medium potatoes

5 green chilies, mild or hot to taste, chopped fine

½ cup chopped fresh coriander leaves (cilantro)

1 teaspoon salt, or to taste

½ cup garbanzo flour

2 cups vegetable oil or ghee for deep-frying

① Soak the tapioca in water *overnight*. Then strain off the water and squeeze the tapioca with your hands to remove any remaining liquid.

② Boil the potatoes until tender. Drain, cool slightly and peel, if desired.

③ Mash the potatoes together with the tapioca. Mix in the chopped green chilies, coriander leaves and salt. Form this mixture into balls, each about ½ inch in diameter.

④ Roll each ball in the garbanzo flour, coating it completely.

⑤ In a thick-bottomed saucepan, heat the vegetable oil or ghee. Carefully immerse the balls in the hot oil, a few at a time, and fry until golden brown. Remove with a slotted spoon, letting the excess oil drip back into the pan. Drain further on paper towels.

Serve hot with chutney.

Yield: 50 potato balls

A Taste of India
SNACKS AND APPETIZERS

Pancakes

The recipes in this section are for savory pancakes that are high in protein and gluten-free.

❦

Garbanzo Flour Pancakes

1 cup garbanzo flour

¼ cup quinoa flour

¼ cup buckwheat flour

¼ cup teff flour

¼ cup miller flour

¼ teaspoon baking soda

1¾ cups water (approximate)

1 cup chopped onions

¾ cup peeled and finely chopped fresh ginger

1 teaspoon minced garlic

1 teaspoon salt

½ teaspoon crushed dry red chilies, or to taste

½ teaspoon oregano (ajwan) seeds

1 tablespoon Kasoon Methi (available at Indian grocers)

olive oil for cooking

① In a large bowl, mix together the five flours and baking soda with enough water to make a pourable batter, being sure that no lumps remain. Add the remaining ingredients and mix well.

② Heat a skillet or flat pan with 1 teaspoon of olive oil. Pour or ladle about ¼ cup of batter into the pan.

③ When the bottom of the pancake is golden brown, flip with a spatula and allow the second side to cook. (When both sides are golden brown; if you want to make it crispy touch each side with oil and cook for 30 seconds more on each side.) Repeat with remaining batter, adding a teaspoon of oil before each ladle of batter.

Serve with yogurt.

Yield: 15 pancakes

A Taste of India
SNACKS AND APPETIZERS

Garbanzo Flour Pancakes with Grated Zucchini

2 cups garbanzo flour

¼ teaspoon baking soda

1¾ cup water (approximate)

1 cup grated zucchini

1 cup chopped onions

¾ cup peeled and finely chopped fresh ginger

1 teaspoon minced garlic

1 teaspoon salt

½ teaspoon crushed dry red chilies, or to taste

½ teaspoon oregano (ajwan) seeds

1 tablespoon Kasoon Methi (available at Indian grocers)

olive oil for cooking

1 In a large bowl, mix together the flour and baking soda with enough water to make a pourable batter, being sure that no lumps remain. Add the remaining ingredients and mix well.

2 Heat a skillet or flat pan with 1 teaspoon of olive oil. Pour or ladle about ¼ cup of batter into the pan.

3 When the bottom of the pancake is golden brown, flip with a spatula and allow the second side to cook. (When both sides are golden brown; if you want to make it crispy, touch each side with oil and cook each side for 30 seconds longer.) Repeat with remaining batter, adding a teaspoon of oil before each ladle of batter.

Serve with yogurt.

Yield: 20 pancakes

A Taste of India
SNACKS AND APPETIZERS

Garbanzo Flour Pancakes with Mashed Potatoes

1 cup garbanzo flour

½ cup mashed potatoes

¼ teaspoon baking soda

1¾ cup water (approximate)

1 cup chopped onions

¾ cup peeled and finely chopped fresh ginger

1 teaspoon minced garlic

1 teaspoon salt

½ teaspoon crushed dry red chilies, or to taste

½ teaspoon oregano (ajwan) seeds

1 tablespoon Kasoon Methi (available at Indian grocers)

olive oil for cooking

❶ In a large bowl, mix together the flour, mashed potatoes and baking soda with enough water to make a pourable batter, being sure that no lumps remain. Add the remaining ingredients and mix well.

❷ Heat a skillet or flat pan with 1 teaspoon of olive oil. Pour or ladle about ¼ cup of batter into the pan.

❸ When the bottom of the pancake is golden brown, flip with a spatula and allow the second side to cook. (When both sides are golden brown; if you want to make it crispy, touch each side with oil and cook each side for 30 seconds longer.) Repeat with remaining batter, adding a teaspoon of oil before each ladle of batter.

Serve with yogurt.

Yield: 12 pancakes

A Taste of India
SNACKS AND APPETIZERS

Garbanzo Flour Pancakes with Mung Bean Flour

1 cup garbanzo flour

1 cup mung bean flour

¼ teaspoon baking soda

1¾ cups water (approximate)

1 cup chopped onions

¾ cup peeled and finely chopped fresh ginger

1 teaspoon minced garlic

1 teaspoon salt

½ teaspoon crushed dry red chilies, or to taste

½ teaspoon oregano (ajwan) seeds

1 tablespoon Kasoon Methi (available at Indian grocers)

① In a large bowl, mix together the two flours and baking soda with enough water to make a pourable batter, being sure that no lumps remain. Add the remaining ingredients and mix well.

② Heat a skillet or flat pan with 1 teaspoon of olive oil. Pour or ladle about ¼ cup of batter into the pan.

③ When the bottom of the pancake is golden brown, flip with a spatula and allow the second side to cook. (When both sides are golden brown; if you want to make it crispy, touch each side with oil and cook each side for 30 seconds longer.) Repeat with remaining batter, adding a teaspoon of oil before each ladle of batter.

Serve with yogurt.

Yield: 16 pancakes

A Taste of India
SNACKS AND APPETIZERS

Tofu Jalapeno Pancakes

Tofu, though not traditionally Indian, adapts itself very well to Indian cooking. These very spicy, hot pancakes are good for cold weather, prevention of flu, and for high energy. They are quite tasty!

2 cups garbanzo flour

1¾ cups water

1 large onion, chopped

½ pound tofu, crumbled

2 large green chilies, mild or hot, to taste

1 teaspoon salt

1 tablespoon oregano (ajwan) seeds

1 head garlic, peeled, cloves chopped fine

¼ cup peeled and finely chopped ginger

2 tablespoons chopped mint leaves

¼–½ cup vegetable oil for frying

 In a large bowl, mix garbanzo flour and water. Add remaining ingredients except oil, and combine well.

 Pour enough oil into a large frying pan to cover the bottom. Heat oil, then lower the heat and ladle in batter to form small pancakes. Cook until pancakes are set and lightly browned on bottom side about 2-3 minutes, then flip and cook until second side is lightly browned. Add oil as necessary every few pancakes.

Serve piping hot with yogurt.

Yield: 12 or more pancakes

A Taste of India
SNACKS AND APPETIZERS

Stuffed Pastry and Biscuits

Vegetable Turnovers
(SAMOSAS)

Good for a formal breakfast, samosas can be made in quantity, kept frozen and then heated in the oven at 350 degrees for a fancy treat on short notice. When hot they will taste freshly made.

For the pastry:

2 cups unbleached white flour

2 teaspoons salt

4 teaspoons melted ghee or olive oil

10-20 tablespoons water

For the filling:

4 medium potatoes

½ teaspoon ground black pepper

3 tablespoons melted ghee or olive oil

1 teaspoon chopped fresh coriander leaves (cilantro)

3 teaspoons ground coriander

To make the pastry:

① In a bowl, sift together the flour and 2 teaspoons of salt. Add the 4 teaspoons of ghee, working it into the flour with your fingertips. Make indention in the center of the flour and slowly add the water, gradually mixing in the flour to form a soft dough. Knead for 5–10 minutes.

② Break off a piece of dough and form into a ball about the size of a walnut. On a lightly floured pastry board or flat surface, roll out the ball with a rolling pin to form a thin, round pancake.

③ Cut this pancake in half and fit the two half-circles thus formed on top of each other. With a fork, press together the round edge, leaving the straight edge open. Keep a damp cloth over the pastry so it doesn't dry out. Repeat with remaining dough.

A Taste of India
SNACKS AND APPETIZERS

3 teaspoons ground cumin

2 tablespoons dry pomegranate seeds

1 teaspoon crushed dry red chilies

6 green chilies, mild or hot, to taste, chopped

1 teaspoon salt, or to taste

¼ cup green peas, fresh or frozen

2 cups vegetable oil or ghee for deep-frying

To make the filling:

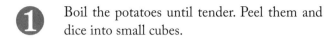 Boil the potatoes until tender. Peel them and dice into small cubes.

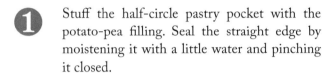 In a large, thick-bottomed frying pan or wok, heat the vegetable oil or ghee and add the remaining filling ingredients, along with the potatoes. Mix thoroughly and cook over low heat for 2 minutes, stirring continuously. Set aside to cool.

To make the turnovers:

1. Stuff the half-circle pastry pocket with the potato-pea filling. Seal the straight edge by moistening it with a little water and pinching it closed.

2. In a deep, thick-bottomed saucepan, heat the 2 cups of vegetable oil or ghee. Turn down the heat and carefully immerse 3–4 turnovers in the oil. Deep-fry over low heat until golden brown for about 2 minutes. Remove from the oil with a slotted spoon, letting the excess oil drip back into the pan. Drain further on paper towels.

Serve hot with chutney or ketchup.

Yield: 16–20 turnovers

A Taste of India
SNACKS AND APPETIZERS

❧

Deep-Fried Bean-Filled Pancakes
(KHASTAA KACHOREE)

Serve as a snack or for breakfast.

For the beans:

½ cup urad dahl (split black mung beans)

1½ cups water for soaking

For the pastry:

1 cup whole-wheat pastry flour

½ teaspoon salt

2 tablespoons ghee and olive oil

¾ cup lukewarm water

For the filling:

2 tablespoons ghee

1 teaspoon red chili powder

3 teaspoons ground coriander

1 teaspoon black cumin seeds

Soak the well-washed beans in 1½ cups of water *overnight*. Then cook them on a medium heat for *2 hours*, or *until soft*.

To make the pastry:

1. In a bowl, sift together the flour and salt. Add the 2 teaspoons of oil and the 2 tablespoons of ghee, working them into the flour with your fingertips. Gradually add ¾ cup of lukewarm water and mix until a lump of dough is formed.

2. Place the dough on a lightly floured pastry board or flat surface and knead for 5 minutes, until smooth and pliable. Break off a small piece of dough and form into a ball approximately 1½ inches in diameter. Repeat using remaining dough. You should have enough dough to make 12 balls. Cover the balls with a damp cloth to keep them from drying out.

To make the filling:

3. In a thick-bottomed frying pan, heat the 2 tablespoons of ghee and sauté chili powder, coriander, cumin, baking soda and 2 teaspoons of water until brown. Then mix in the cooked dahl and stir thoroughly. Remove from the heat and cool.

A Taste of India
SNACKS AND APPETIZERS

¼ teaspoon baking soda

2 teaspoons water

2 cups vegetable oil or ghee for deep-frying

To make the filled pancakes:

 Lightly dust a pastry board or flat surface with flour. Using a rolling pin, roll out one ball of dough. Place a portion of the filling in the center, then fold the sides of the dough up over the filling. Using your hands, carefully press the filled ball out into a pancake about 3 inches in diameter.

 In a thick-bottomed saucepan, heat the 2 cups of vegetable oil or ghee, turn down to medium heat. Carefully immerse a pancake in the hot oil and deep-fry until golden brown 2-3 minutes. Remove with a slotted spoon, letting the excess oil drip back into the pan. Drain pancake on paper towels. Repeat with remaining pancakes. Serve hot.

Yield: 12 stuffed pancakes

A Taste of India
SNACKS AND APPETIZERS

Punjabi-Style Bean-Filled Pancakes
(PUNJAABEE KACHOREE)

For breakfast, snack or a special luncheon.

For the beans:

⅔ cups pink lentils

1½ cups water

For the pastry:

½ cup unbleached white flour

⅓ cup warm water

½ teaspoon salt

3 teaspoons yogurt

¼ cup ghee or vegetable oil

For the filling:

¼ teaspoon baking soda

2 teaspoons red chili powder

½ teaspoon salt

2 teaspoons ground coriander

2 teaspoons ground black cumin

2 tablespoons ghee

To prepare the beans:

Soak the well-washed pink lentils in 1½ cups water for 3-4 hours.

To make the pastry:

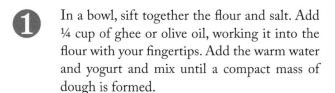
In a bowl, sift together the flour and salt. Add ¼ cup of ghee or olive oil, working it into the flour with your fingertips. Add the warm water and yogurt and mix until a compact mass of dough is formed.

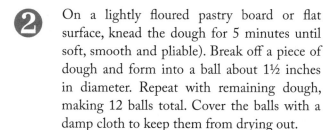
On a lightly floured pastry board or flat surface, knead the dough for 5 minutes until soft, smooth and pliable). Break off a piece of dough and form into a ball about 1½ inches in diameter. Repeat with remaining dough, making 12 balls total. Cover the balls with a damp cloth to keep them from drying out.

To make the filling:

Lightly dust a pastry board or flat surface with flour. Using a rolling pin, roll a ball of dough into a 6-inch circle. Place a portion of the filling in the center, then fold the sides of the dough up, over the filling. Using your hands, carefully press the filled ball into a pancake about 3 inches in diameter.

A Taste of India
SNACKS AND APPETIZERS

2 teaspoons farina (plain Cream of Wheat)

For the pancakes:

¼ cup flour for dusting

2 cups olive oil or ghee for deep-frying

 In a thick-bottomed saucepan, heat the olive oil or ghee, turn down to medium heat. Carefully immerse a pancake in the hot oil and deep-fry until golden brown, about 2–3 minutes. Remove with a slotted spoon, letting the excess oil drip back into the pan. Drain further on paper towels. Repeat with remaining pancakes. Serve hot.

Yield: 12 stuffed pancakes

A Taste of India
SNACKS AND APPETIZERS

Party Wafers
(GOLGAPPAS)

These wafers are a flaky appetizer or side dish. Serve with Jaljeera

¾ cup whole-wheat pastry flour

4 teaspoons farina

½ cup water

¼ cup flour for dusting pastry board

2 cups olive oil or ghee for deep-frying

1 In a bowl, mix together the flour and the farina. Gradually add the water, mixing to form a lump of dough. Knead the dough until soft and pliable for 5–10 minutes.

2 Place the dough on a lightly floured pastry board or flat surface and roll it out into a long, thin loaf with your hands. Cut off small pieces, about the size of an almond, and form these, either with your hands or with a rolling pin, into small, thin, disk-shaped rounds. Cover them with a damp cloth to keep them from drying out.

3 In a thick-bottomed saucepan, heat the olive oil or ghee to smoking point and deep-fry the pastry rounds 3 or 4 at a time. They will quickly puff up and pop to the surface when done. Scoop out with a slotted spoon, letting the excess oil drip back into the pan.

4 These wafers (*golgappas*) are served by making a small hole in the side and filling with a couple of cooked chickpeas then pouring Jaljeera into the hole. Those rounds that do not puff up are called paparies and are equally delicious.

Yield: about 32 wafers

A Taste of India
SNACKS AND APPETIZERS

Deep-Fried Biscuits
(MATHEE)

A really scrumptious snack at home or for the road. Good eaten hot with jam.

1 cup unbleached white flour

6 tablespoons water

1 teaspoon salt

¼ cup flour for dusting pastry board

½ teaspoon oregano (ajwan) seeds

3 tablespoons melted ghee

2 cups olive oil or ghee for deep-frying

① In a bowl, sift together the flour and salt. Add the oregano seeds and mix thoroughly. Add the melted ghee, working it into the flour with your fingertips until the flour is like dry crumbs. Gradually add the water, mixing until a stiff dough is formed.

② Place the dough on a lightly floured pastry board or flat surface and knead for 5 minutes. Break off a small piece of dough the size of an almond. With a rolling pin, roll these pieces out into little disks about 3 inches in diameter. These disks (some of which might be actually triangular in shape) will be cracked around the edges.

③ In a thick-bottomed saucepan, heat the olive oil or ghee, then turn down the heat to medium. Immerse the disks in the hot oil 3–4 at a time and deep-fry, turning frequently, until golden brown about 2 minutes. Remove with a slotted spoon, letting the excess oil drip back into the pan. Drain further on paper towels. Stored in an airtight container, they will keep unrefrigerated for 8-10 weeks.

Yield: 12–16 three-inch-wide biscuits

A Taste of India
SNACKS AND APPETIZERS

Punjabi-Style Deep-Fried Biscuits
(PUNJAABEE MATHEE)

For breakfast, a take-along snack, or with tea or coffee. Rich and spicy.

1 cup unbleached white flour

¼ teaspoon baking soda

1 teaspoon black peppercorns, crushed

¼ cup melted ghee

½ cup water

½ teaspoon oregano (ajwan) seeds

2 teaspoons yogurt

1 teaspoon salt

¼ cup flour for dusting pastry board

2 cups vegetable oil or ghee for deep-frying

1 Sift the flour into a bowl. Add the crushed black peppercorns, oregano seeds, salt and baking soda and mix well. Add the melted ghee and work it into the flour with your fingertips. Add the water and yogurt and mix thoroughly, forming a stiff dough.

2 Place the dough on a lightly floured pastry board or flat surface and knead for a few minutes. Break off small pieces of dough to form 12 balls. With a rolling pin, roll each dough ball into a thick biscuit, approximately 2 inches in diameter.

3 In a thick-bottomed saucepan, heat the 2 cups of vegetable oil or ghee until smoking. Remove from the heat. Immerse the biscuits in the oil and let them fry, off the heat, for 5 minutes. Return the pan to a low heat and turn the biscuits over. Fry until golden brown. Remove the pan from the heat again and let them fry a few more minutes off the heat. Turn them again and return the pan to the heat. When the biscuits are brown, remove from the oil with a slotted spoon, letting the excess oil drip back into the pan. Drain further on paper towels.

Yield: 12 biscuits

A Taste of India
SNACKS AND APPETIZERS

Rich Salted Biscuits
(KHASTAA MATHEE)

1 cup unbleached white flour

6 teaspoons butter, chilled

1½ teaspoons baking powder

7-9 teaspoons milk

1 teaspoon honey

½ teaspoon salt

¼ cup flour for dusting pastry board

½ teaspoon onion seeds or oregano (ajwan) seeds

¼ cup milk for brushing

1 In a bowl, sift together the flour, baking powder and salt. Add the butter, working it in with your fingertips. Mix in the milk and honey, forming a firm dough.

2 On a lightly floured pastry board or flat surface, roll the dough out into a ½-inch-thick slab. Cut into rounds with a cookie cutter. Prick the top of each round with a fork.

3 Brush the top of each biscuit with a little milk (from the ¼ cup) and sprinkle with onion seeds. Place on an ungreased cookie sheet and bake in a 300 degree oven 15 minutes or until golden brown.

Yield: 16 small biscuits

A Taste of India
SNACKS AND APPETIZERS

Stuffed Pastry and Biscuits

⚜

Banana with Chat Masala

An exotic evening snack, this is good served with Yogi Tea, other salty snacks, or a sweet snack to balance the taste.

1 banana

2 pinches of chat masala

Juice of 1 lemon

1 Peel the banana and cut in half lengthwise.

2 Squeeze the lemon juice onto each banana half and sprinkle with chat masala.

Chat masala can be purchased in Indian food stores or made fresh. To make chat masala: Mix together ¾ teaspoon ground roasted cumin seeds, ¼ teaspoon ground black pepper, ¼ teaspoon red chili powder, ¼ teaspoon ground asafoetida, ¼ teaspoon mango powder, ½ teaspoon black salt and ¾ teaspoon kosher or coarse salt.

Yield: serves 1–2

A Taste of India
SNACKS AND APPETIZERS

Spicy Cashews and Peanuts
(MASAALAA KAAJOO EE MOONGPHOOLEE)

A "ready mix" to store or take anywhere.

2 teaspoons mango powder

¼ teaspoon black salt

¾ teaspoon ground black pepper

½ teaspoon salt

2 teaspoons ground cumin

½ teaspoon red chili powder

½ of a whole clove, crushed

¼ cup ghee for frying

½ pound (1⅓ cups) raw peanuts, shelled

½ pound (1½ cups) cashew nuts

Preheat the oven to 275 degrees.

① In a bowl, mix together the mango powder, black pepper, red chili, black salt, regular salt, ground cumin and crushed clove.

② In a thick-bottomed frying pan, heat half of the ghee and fry the cashews over low heat until golden about 2–3 minutes. Remove the cashews, add more ghee if necessary, and fry the peanuts until golden. (When frying nuts, stir constantly and keep a sharp eye; they start to burn very suddenly.)

③ Transfer the fried cashews and peanuts to a bowl and immediately sprinkle with the spice mixture, tossing until all the nuts are well coated.

④ Pour the nut mixture into a large brown paper bag and shake well. Remove the nuts from the bag with a medium-sized strainer and place on a cookie sheet. (Excess spice mixture can be discarded or stored for future use.)

⑤ Bake the nuts for 5–8 minutes or until crisp. Store in a sealed container at room temperature and use within 2–3 weeks.

Yield: about 3 cups

A Taste of India
SNACKS AND APPETIZERS

❦

Curried Cheese Cubes
(MASAALAA PANIR)

1 cup panir

⅛ teaspoon ground red chili (mild)

2 teaspoons mango powder (or lemon juice)

⅛ teaspoon ground turmeric

½ teaspoon salt, or to taste

1 tablespoon ground ginger blended with 1 tablespoon water

2 teaspoons garbanzo flour

2 cups vegetable oil or ghee for deep-frying

1 Cut panir into cubes about 1 inch.

2 Mix together red chili, turmeric, ginger/water, mango powder (or lemon juice) and salt. Sprinkle over panir cubes evenly until well coated.

3 Lightly dust each cube with garbanzo flour.

4 In a thick-bottomed saucepan or wok, heat the vegetable oil or ghee. Carefully immerse 3-5 panir cubes into the oil, deep-frying until brown. Remove with a slotted spoon, letting the excess oil drip back into the pan. Drain cubes on paper towels. Serve hot, with chutney or hot sauce.

Yield: 15 one-inch-square cubes

King Janak Plans a Feast

Inspirational stories like this one are among those that were told to me as a child and helped to shape my attitudes toward the art of preparing food.

Janak, who ruled much of India in ancient times, was known as both the greatest king and the greatest yogi. It is said that to celebrate his fiftieth birthday he arranged a spectacular feast, the likes of which had never been seen before. Months in advance, he dispatched his royal cooks to all parts of the known world to collect the most delectable recipes that each region had to offer. Then he sent invitations to all the kings, princes and noblemen, to the greatest holy men and seers, and to representatives of the people in the villages and farm lands.

When the guests arrived at the great hall, they were astounded by the great variety and quantity of food that King Janak had set before them. Along the perimeters of the hall were long banquet tables, each of them filled with a colorful array of dishes from different regions. There was Italian food, Greek food, Arabian food; Persian, Tibetan and Chinese food; African food and Thai food; and of course a variety of delicacies from all over India. But the greatest astonishment was King Janak himself.

Seated on a dais with an eminent collection of heads of state, leaders of religious sects and honest, hardworking people of the villages, King Janak enjoyed his own meal—a half-filled bowl of rice with homemade yogurt. When asked why he abstained from the meal of a lifetime which he himself had arranged, King Janak stood up and replied, "I gathered together all the most delicious foods from all over the world and brought them to this meal just to honor all of you, my friends. Then I gathered together all of my training, all of my discipline, and all of my self-restraint and brought those things to this meal as well. In this way I have honored myself."

VEGETABLE DISHES

Vegetables dishes (sabji or subzi) are center stage in the theater of Indian food preparation. With the vast majority of the country's people strictly vegetarian, India has, over thousands of years, developed a vegetarian cuisine unequaled anywhere else in the world. The purpose of Indian vegetarian cooking is not to simulate the taste and appearance of meat but to raise the presentation of the essential vegetable to its highest potential. Vegetables are prepared so that their aroma is extraordinary, they look exquisite, taste delicious and are hearty, satisfying and nourishing.

There are four major ways of preparing vegetable main dishes in India. In planning a meal with several dishes, it is nice to have a dish from each of these categories:

The "wet" way means with sauce (*kari*). This is what is commonly referred to as curry. Curry powder, as sold in the stores, is almost never used in its preparation. Wet vegetable dishes usually contain two or more vegetables cooked or stewed together in a highly flavored, though not necessarily spicy, sauce. Sometimes the vegetables are in the form of balls (koftas), which have been deep-fried before being cooked in the sauce.

The "dry" way means there is no sauce. These are *bhujia* or *bhajia*. The vegetables are cooked by sautéing or frying with spices in a little ghee or vegetable oil. In a "dry" dish the onions and ginger would be sliced or chopped rather than grated or powdered.

Stuffed vegetables. Stuffed vegetables are just that: sturdy vegetables such as peppers, melons, even potatoes, that are scooped out, stuffed with a spice mixture and then fried or baked.

A Taste of India
VEGETABLE DISHES

Vegetables with rice or beans. Vegetables may either be cooked right along with the rice or beans, or cooked separately and added later on. Bean dishes (*dahls*) provide much of the protein of the Indian vegetarian diet, while rice dishes (*pilau, pullao* or *baryani*) provide healthy carbohydrates. The recipes for rice and bean dishes are in separate chapters.

A Taste of India
VEGETABLE DISHES

Potato Cream Rolls
(MAKHNEE AALOO TIKKEE)

For the potato rolls:

2 medium potatoes

1 teaspoon salt

1 teaspoon ghee

1 tablespoon fresh coriander

½ teaspoon crushed dry red chilies

leaves (cilantro), chopped

3 green chilies, mild or hot, to taste, chopped fine

½ teaspoon salt

¼ cup cream

2 teaspoons peeled, finely chopped fresh ginger

For the batter:

2 tablespoons unbleached white flour

2 tablespoons water

2 tablespoons fine bread crumbs for dusting

2 cups vegetable oil or ghee for deep-frying

1 Boil the potatoes until tender in water with 1 teaspoon of salt added to it. Remove the potatoes from the water and set aside to cool. Peel and grate them.

2 In a large, thick-bottomed frying pan, heat the butter and add the red and green chilies, chopped ginger, coriander leaves and ½ teaspoon salt. Mix in the grated potatoes and cook for 1 minute. Add cream, mix well and set aside.

3 Make a thin batter of the flour and water. Flour your hands, take a handful of the potato mixture, and form into a small roll. Dip this roll in the batter, then dust it with the bread crumbs. Repeat with remaining potato mixture.

4 In a thick-bottomed saucepan or wok, heat the vegetable oil or ghee for deep frying. Carefully slip 3-4 rolls into the hot oil and deep-fry on a low heat until golden brown for about 2 minutes. Remove with a slotted spoon, letting the excess oil drip back into the pan. Drain further on paper towels. Serve hot.

Yield: 24 potato rolls

A Taste of India
VEGETABLE DISHES

Onion and Tomato Curry
(PIAAZ TAMAATAR SABJEE)

A pungent and colorful side dish.

1 tablespoon vegetable oil or ghee

5 cloves garlic, chopped

1-inch piece fresh ginger, peeled and chopped fine

½ pound onions, sliced thin

5 green chilies, mild or hot, to taste, chopped

1 teaspoon cumin seeds

¼ teaspoon salt, or to taste

½ teaspoon ground turmeric

1 small tomato, sliced thin

½ teaspoon garam masala

 In a large, thick-bottomed frying pan or wok, heat the oil or ghee and sauté the onions, garlic and ginger until light brown. (Add a little water, if necessary, to prevent dehydration while cooking.)

 Add the green chilies, turmeric, garam masala, cumin and salt and stir well. Next, add the tomato and cook over low heat until the oil starts to separate out, about 10–15 minutes. (If mixture starts to stick, add a little water.)

Yield: 1½ cups

A Taste of India
VEGETABLE DISHES

Eggplant Bhartha
(BAIGAN BHARTHAA)

1 very large eggplant or 2 small eggplants

2 teaspoons vegetable oil or ghee

2 large tomatoes, chopped

1 teaspoon ground cumin

1 large onion, chopped

¼ teaspoon salt, or to taste

1-inch piece fresh ginger, peeled and chopped fine

1/8 teaspoon ground black pepper, or to taste

1 In the oven, broil the eggplant until the peel is charred and the inside is soft, turning eggplant occasionally so that all sides char evenly. Let it cool, peel, and mash the pulp. Set aside.

2 In a large, thick-bottomed frying pan, heat the vegetable oil or ghee and sauté the onions and ginger until the onions are golden, stirring frequently so that the ginger doesn't stick. Add the tomatoes, cumin, salt and black pepper and continue to fry until the tomatoes are mushy. (Add water, if necessary, to prevent dehydration.)

3 Add the mashed eggplant and cook, stirring often, until the oil begins to separate out from the vegetables, about 10-15 minutes. Serve hot.

Yield: 2 cups

A Taste of India
VEGETABLE DISHES

❧

Stewed Tomatoes
(TAMAATAR BHARTHAA)

4 ripe tomatoes

1 teaspoon salt, or to taste

1 large onion, chopped

1 tablespoon honey, or to taste

2-3 green chilies, mild or hot to taste, chopped

① Immerse the tomatoes briefly in boiling water; the skins will shrivel up. Remove from the water and peel off the skins. In a bowl, mash the peeled tomatoes with a fork, removing any hard parts.

② Add the onion and green chilies, then the salt and honey, and mix thoroughly.

Yield: 4 cups

❧

Green Chili Stew

8 or 9 fresh long green chilies

3 tablespoons olive oil

2 large onions, chopped

1 large tomato, chopped

Preheat oven to 450 degrees.

① Place chilies on a baking tray and roast in oven for 10–12 minutes, turning chilies so all sides are brown.

② Transfer the roasted chilies to a bowl and wash them with water. Peel off the skins and partially mash the chilies. Set aside.

③ Warm the olive oil in a skillet over medium heat. Add the onions and sauté until light brown. Add tomato and the lightly mashed chilies and sauté all together 3–5 minutes.

Yield: 4 servings

A Taste of India
VEGETABLE DISHES

Chickpea Dahl Curry
(CHANAA DAAL KAREE)

This spicy, satisfying dish is an unusual blend of flavors. Serve with plain rice.

½ cup lotus root

7 cups water

½ cup chickpeas (garbanzo beans)

½ cup cubed peeled eggplant

1 tomato, chopped

12 green chilies, mild or hot, to taste, chopped fine

½ cup diced cauliflower

1 teaspoon salt, or to taste

½ cup green peas, fresh or frozen

2 teaspoons ground turmeric

1 teaspoon crushed dry red chilies

½ cup ghee or vegetable oil

2 teaspoons mustard seeds

 If the lotus root is dry, it should be soaked overnight. (Canned lotus root need not be soaked.) Also, clean and soak the chickpeas in 7 cups of water overnight. In the morning, wash, peel and cut the lotus root into small pieces. Cook the chickpeas in the water in which they were soaked, along with the lotus root pieces. When the chickpeas have become very soft, remove the lotus root pieces from the water and set them aside in a bowl. Strain off the water from the chickpeas (don't throw the water away, though!) and set aside.

 In a large, thick-bottomed pot, place the chickpeas, 8 cups of water (including chickpea water), salt, turmeric, red chilies, and all the vegetables except the lotus root. Cook over low heat until all the vegetables are soft. Add the cooked lotus root.

A Taste of India
VEGETABLE DISHES

2 teaspoons fenugreek seeds

2 teaspoons cumin seeds

½ cup tamarind concentrate, seedless

4 teaspoons chopped fresh coriander leaves (cilantro)

③ In a thick-bottomed frying pan, heat the vegetable oil or ghee and sauté the fenugreek seeds, mustard seeds and cumin seeds. Add the tamarind and coriander leaves and cook for 5 minutes. Pour this mixture over the chickpea-vegetable mixture and serve.

Yield: 8 cups

Leek Bhajia

A mild complement, sweet and light, for any meal.

2 medium leeks

1 teaspoon ground turmeric

2 teaspoons butter

½ teaspoon ground ginger

½ teaspoon cumin seeds

¼ teaspoon salt, or to taste

½ teaspoon garam masala

① Carefully wash the leeks to remove any sand. Slice the whole leek into thin rounds and soak in water for 10 minutes. Rinse thoroughly and drain off all the water.

② In a thick-bottomed frying pan or wok, melt the butter and add the cumin seeds, sautéing for a few seconds (making sure they don't burn). Add the turmeric, ginger, salt and leeks. Continue to fry 3–4 minutes, then add a little water, cover and cook over low heat until the leeks are tender about 3 minutes longer.

③ Drain off any water and sprinkle the leeks with garam masala before serving.

Yield: 2 cups

A Taste of India
VEGETABLE DISHES

Chickpea-Flour Curry
(SINDHEE KAREE)

A mild curry with interesting textures. Serve with plain rice and a spicy chutney.

2 large lotus roots

2 tablespoons tamarind concentrate (seedless)

4 tablespoons warm water

2 potatoes

½ head cauliflower

1 small eggplant

2-3 tablespoons vegetable oil or ghee

¾ cup chickpea (garbanzo) flour

4 cups water

¾ teaspoon salt, or to taste

2 tablespoons ground turmeric

1 tablespoon vegetable oil or ghee

4 whole dried red chilies

① If the lotus root is dry, soak it in water overnight.

② Dissolve the tamarind concentrate in 4 tablespoons of warm water.

③ Wash the potatoes and cut into large pieces. Peel the eggplant and cut into medium pieces. Wash the cauliflower and divide into medium-size flowerets. Scrape and wash the lotus root and cut into big pieces. Wash again thoroughly. Set the vegetables aside.

④ In a large, thick-bottomed saucepan, heat 2–3 tablespoons of vegetable oil or ghee and fry the chickpea flour until light brown, being careful not to let it burn. Slowly add 4 cups water, *stirring continuously* to avoid lumping, and add the turmeric, salt and lotus root. Continue cooking on medium heat until half the liquid is gone.

A Taste of India
VEGETABLE DISHES

2 tablespoons chopped fresh coriander

1 tablespoon fenugreek seeds

leaves (cilantro)

2 teaspoons white cumin seeds

a few fresh mint leaves, chopped

½ cup green peas, fresh or frozen

1 large tomato, chopped

3 green chilies, mild or hot, to taste, chopped

2 tablespoons vegetable oil or ghee

1 tablespoon mustard seeds

5 In a thick-bottomed frying pan, heat the 1 tablespoon of oil or ghee and fry the fenugreek seeds and white cumin seeds until brown. Add them to the chickpea-flour sauce, along with the potatoes, eggplant, cauliflower, peas, green chilies, red chilies, and fresh coriander leaves. Next, add the mint leaves, chopped tomatoes and tamarind water. Simmer for a few minutes.

6 In the same thick-bottomed frying pan you used earlier, heat the 2 tablespoons of oil or ghee and fry the mustard seeds until they start popping. Add to the curry, mixing thoroughly.

Yield: 6 cups

A Taste of India
VEGETABLE DISHES

Creamy Spinach and Cheese
(SAAG PANEER)

Tofu can be used as a simple, though less authentic, substitute.

2 tablespoons ghee

1½ cups panir (or 1½ pounds tofu)

1 tablespoon ghee

5 cloves garlic

1 cup chopped onion

2 whole cloves

1 tablespoon ground ginger

1 cup water

¼ teaspoon baking soda

2½ pounds (4 large bunches) spinach, washed and chopped

1 teaspoon salt, or to taste

½ cup water

1 teaspoon red chili powder

3 medium tomatoes, peeled and chopped

1 Cut the panir into small cubes. In a large, thick-bottomed saucepan, heat 2 tablespoons of ghee and fry the panir gently until light brown. Remove the panir with a slotted spoon, letting the excess ghee drip back into the pan. Set aside.

2 Add 1 tablespoon ghee and fry the onions until transparent. Add the ginger, garlic, cloves and 1 cup of water. Mix thoroughly and cook until the water evaporates.

3 Add the baking soda, salt to taste, ½ cup of water and chopped spinach. Mix thoroughly and cook for 5 minutes.

A Taste of India
VEGETABLE DISHES

2 teaspoons ground cumin

2 teaspoons ground coriander

½ cup cottage cheese

1/8 teaspoon ground nutmeg

½ cup water

 Add the chili powder, cumin, coriander, nutmeg, tomatoes, cottage cheese, fried panir and another ½ cup water. Cook over low heat until the panir is soft and the ghee begins to separate out, about 3 minutes.

Yield: 6 cups

A Taste of India
VEGETABLE DISHES

Ripe Mango Curry
(AMB DEE SABJEE)

Delicious and spicy, with an unusual blend of tastes.

4 large ripe mangoes

2 tablespoons vegetable oil or ghee

4 whole dry red chilies

1 cup grated fresh coconut

1 teaspoon mustard seeds

1 teaspoon ground turmeric

1½ cups water

1 tablespoon honey

¼ cup raisins

2 bay leaves

4 whole cloves

½ teaspoon salt, or to taste

1 Peel the mangoes and cut into small pieces.

2 In a large, thick-bottomed frying pan or wok, heat the oil or ghee and fry the mustard seeds and red chilies until they start to snap and crackle, being careful not to let them burn. Mix in the grated coconut and turmeric and fry until light brown, stirring continuously.

3 Add the mangoes, water, raisins, cloves, honey, bay leaves and salt. Simmer over low heat for 10 minutes, stirring occasionally.

Yield: 8 cups

Note: This dish may be reheated and served the following day, when it will taste spicier.

A Taste of India
VEGETABLE DISHES

Pineapple Curry
(ANAANAAS SABJEE)

An exotic side dish, easy to prepare and good with plain rice.

1 teaspoon coriander seeds

½ teaspoon mustard seeds

4 whole, dry red chilies

1 large onion, chopped

2 tablespoons vegetable oil or ghee

1 large pineapple, peeled and cut into small pieces

½ teaspoon salt, or to taste

1 pint water

2 tablespoons honey

1 With a mortar and pestle or a coffee grinder, grind the coriander seeds and red chilies to a paste.

2 In a large, thick-bottomed frying pan or wok, heat the vegetable oil or ghee and fry the mustard seeds and onion until light brown. Add the coriander/chili paste and stir well.

3 Add the pineapple pieces and stir well. Add the honey, salt and water. Cook over low heat until the sauce is thickened.

Yield: 4 cups

A Taste of India
VEGETABLE DISHES

Yam Curry
(ARBEE BHUJIAA)

Yams with a distinctly Indian flavor.

2 medium-size yams, peeled

2 tablespoons oregano (ajwan) seeds

½ tablespoon ghee

1/3 tablespoon ghee

1 teaspoon garam masala

1½ teaspoon ground turmeric

2-3 green chilies, mild or hot, to taste, chopped fine

1 tablespoon white cumin seeds

½ teaspoon salt, or to taste

1 teaspoon peeled and finely chopped fresh ginger

¼ teaspoon ground black pepper

5 teaspoons mango powder

1 Boil or bake the yams until tender but not mushy. Peel, then flatten each whole yam by pressing with your hands (or slice).

2 Sprinkle the yams with oregano seeds. In a large frying pan, heat ½ tablespoon of ghee and fry the yams until they are golden brown.

3 Add 1/3 tablespoon of ghee to the pan. Mix in the turmeric, white cumin, garam masala, ginger, green chilies, salt and black pepper. Cook for 2–3 minutes.

4 When ready to serve, add the mango powder and cook for another minute or two.

A Taste of India
VEGETABLE DISHES

Garnish:

1 small tomato, chopped

2 teaspoons chopped fresh coriander leaves (cilantro)

 Place on a serving dish and garnish with chopped tomato and coriander leaves.

Yield: 2 cups

A Taste of India

VEGETABLE DISHES

Royal Potato Curry

(SHAAHEE AALOO SABJEE)

Fresh coconut and coriander make this dish a delight.

For the potato balls:

6 medium potatoes

1 teaspoon salt

water for boiling the potatoes

1 tablespoon ghee, melted

1 teaspoon ground ginger

2 green chilies, mild or hot, to taste, chopped very fine

½ teaspoon salt, or to taste

2 cups vegetable oil or ghee for deep-frying

4 tablespoons unbleached white flour

For the curry:

2 teaspoons white poppy seeds

water to cover poppy seeds

To make the potato balls:

1 Boil the potatoes in water with 1 teaspoon salt until tender. Remove from the water, peel and mash. Set aside to cool.

2 Add the tablespoon of melted ghee, green chilies, ground ginger and ½ teaspoon salt and mix thoroughly. Form this mixture into small balls, each about the size of a walnut.

3 In a bowl, add enough water to the flour to make a thin batter. Dip the potato balls in the batter.

4 In a thick-bottomed saucepan, heat the 2 cups of vegetable oil or ghee to smoking point. Carefully immerse the potato balls in the hot oil and fry until brown. Remove with a slotted spoon, letting the excess oil drip back into the pan. Drain the balls further on paper towels.

To make the curry:

1 Soak the white poppy seeds for 10 minutes in just enough water to cover them.

2 In an electric blender, whirl the white poppy seeds for a few seconds, then add the green cardamom seeds, almonds, coconut and milk.

A Taste of India
VEGETABLE DISHES

4 green cardamom pods (use only the seeds)

2 tablespoons grated coconut (fresh, if possible)

2 tablespoons almonds

3-4 cups milk

1 tablespoon cornstarch

3 green chilies, mild or hot, to taste

2 small tomatoes, chopped

½ teaspoon salt, or to taste

½ teaspoon red chili powder

½ teaspoon ground white pepper

2 teaspoons chopped fresh coriander leaves(cilantro)

③ Transfer this mixture to a thick-bottomed saucepan or wok and bring to a boil. Mix the cornstarch with enough milk (from step 2) to form a paste, and then add this paste to the rest of the boiling milk, mixing thoroughly. Continue cooking and stirring until the sauce thickens.

④ When thick, add the green chili powder, red chili powder, white pepper and tomatoes and stir well. Add the fried potato balls, mixing them in carefully so they don't break. Add ½ teaspoon of salt. Garnish with chopped coriander leaves.

Yield: approximately 48 balls and 5 cups of curry

A Taste of India
VEGETABLE DISHES

Kashmiri Steamed Potatoes
(KASHMEEREE DUM AALOO)

Delicate and distinctive in flavor, these potatoes are a gourmet delight!

1 teaspoon red chili powder

1 teaspoon chopped fresh coriander

1 teaspoon ground ginger

1 teaspoon fresh coriander, chopped

1 teaspoon ground anise seed

1 teaspoon ground turmeric

½ teaspoon salt

2 green chilies, mild or hotto taste, chopped fine

¾ teaspoon garam masala

pinch of ground nutmeg

8 very small potatoes

½ cup mustard oil

1. Measure out chili powder, ground ginger, ground anise seed, chopped coriander leaves, turmeric and salt and set aside in a small bowl.

2. In a separate bowl, mix together chopped chilies, garam masala and nutmeg.

3. Boil the potatoes. When tender, remove from the water, peel and set aside.

4. Reserve 2 tablespoons mustard oil. In a thick-bottomed frying pan or wok, heat the remaining mustard oil until smoking. Fry the whole boiled potatoes until golden brown. Remove from the oil and prick them all over with a toothpick. Discard oil from pan and wipe the pan clean with a paper towel.

5. In a frying pan, heat 2 tablespoons of mustard oil reserved earlier. Remove from the heat and add the asafoetida and stir until it swells. Then crush it to a powder and reheat, adding the bowl of chili powder, ginger, anise, coriander, turmeric and salt.

6. In a bowl, beat the yogurt slightly to thicken it, then add to the spice mixture along with ½ cup of water. Simmer for 15 minutes.

A Taste of India
VEGETABLE DISHES

pinch of asafoetida

¾ cup yogurt

½ cup water

7 Add the potatoes and continue to simmer over low heat until the sauce thickens, about 10 minutes. Sprinkle with garam masala, ground nutmeg and green chili mixture before serving.

Yield: 2½ cups

Dry Potato Curry
(SUBHAA AALOO SABJEE)

Best served with yogurt.

3 medium potatoes, peeled and cubed

6 tablespoons vegetable oil or ghee

2 teaspoons cumin seeds

1 teaspoon crushed dry red chilies

2 teaspoons mustard seeds

2 teaspoons oregano (ajwan) seeds

½ teaspoon salt, or to taste

a few fresh coriander leaves (cilantro)

1 Steam the cubed potatoes until tender. Set aside.

2 In a large thick-bottomed frying pan or wok, heat the vegetable oil or ghee, then add the mustard, oregano and cumin seeds. Stir well and add the red chilies and salt.

3 Add the steamed potatoes, continuing to stir as they cook for a few minutes longer. Garnish with coriander leaves before serving.

Yield: 2 cups

A Taste of India
VEGETABLE DISHES

Potato and Tomato Curry
(AALOO TAMAATAR SABJEE)

3 medium potatoes

water to cover potatoes

4 tablespoons vegetable oil or ghee

2 tablespoons peeled and finely chopped fresh ginger

2 large onions, sliced

1 teaspoon ground turmeric

1 teaspoon cumin seeds

1 teaspoon red chili powder

2 medium tomatoes, chopped

1 teaspoon salt

2 cups water

2 teaspoons garam masala

a few fresh coriander leaves (cilantro)

1. Peel the potatoes and dice. Keep them immersed in cold water to prevent discoloration.

2. In a large thick-bottomed frying pan, heat the vegetable oil or ghee. Add the onions and ginger and sauté until golden brown. Add the turmeric, red chili powder, cumin seeds and tomatoes. Mix thoroughly and fry for 2 minutes.

3. Add the potato cubes and fry for 1 minute, stirring continuously. Next, add the salt and water and simmer over low heat until the potatoes are soft and start to crumble about 1 more minute. A thick sauce will form. Sprinkle with garam masala and garnish with coriander leaves.

Yield: 3 cups

A Taste of India
VEGETABLE DISHES

String Beans and Potatoes
(FALEEAAN AALOO)

This dish is very hardy and satisfying. It goes well with tomato curry.

⅓–½ cup vegetable oil or ghee

1 inch peeled and finely chopped fresh ginger

1 onion, chopped

½ teaspoon ground turmeric

½ pound green beans (string beans) (about 1½ cups)

½ teaspoon crushed dry red chilies

½ cup water

3 green chilies, mild or hot, to taste, chopped

1 medium potato, peeled and diced

½ teaspoon salt, or to taste

½ teaspoon ground coriander

① In a large thick-bottomed saucepan, heat the vegetable oil or ghee and sauté the onions and ginger until light brown.

② One by one, add the turmeric, crushed dry red chilies, green chilies, and salt, stirring after each addition. Add the green beans, ½ cup water and potatoes and cook until potatoes are tender, about 10 minutes. If necessary, add a little more water and cook until it is a "dry" vegetable mixture.

③ Stir for 1 minute, sprinkle with coriander and let sit for 5 minutes.

Yield: 4 cups

A Taste of India
VEGETABLE DISHES

Green Pea Dishes

❦

Mushroom and Pea Curry
(KHUMBAA MATAR)

A very tasty dish!

¼ cup vegetable oil or ghee

1-inch piece fresh ginger, peeled and chopped fine

2 large onions, sliced

5 cloves garlic, chopped

½ teaspoon ground turmeric

1 teaspoon salt, or to taste

½ teaspoon red chili powder

3 medium tomatoes, chopped, or 2 tablespoons tomato paste

1 tablespoon garam masala

¼ teaspoon ground nutmeg

① In a large thick-bottomed saucepan or wok, heat the oil or ghee and sauté the onions, garlic and ginger until golden brown. Add the turmeric, red chili powder, garam masala, nutmeg and salt and stir well. Next, add the tomatoes or tomato paste and continue cooking and stirring until the oil begins to separate out about 1 minute.

② Add the mushrooms and mix well. Add the water, cover and cook over medium heat for 2 minutes. Add the peas, mix well and cover. Simmer over low heat, being careful not to let the mixture burn.

A Taste of India
VEGETABLE DISHES

½ pound mushrooms (about 18 medium-sized) washed and sliced

1 cup water

½ pound green peas, fresh or frozen (about 1½ cups)

❸ After all the liquid is gone, continue cooking, stirring continuously, until the oil starts to separate out. Remove from the heat and serve.

Yield: 4–5 cups

A Taste of India
VEGETABLE DISHES

Pea and Potato Curry
(AALOO MATAR)

A nice dish for formal occasions.

1 pound (about 3 cups) green peas, fresh or frozen (defrosted)

½ teaspoon crushed dry red chilies

1 teaspoon garam masala

1 medium potato, boiled and peeled

½ cup chickpea (garbanzo) flour

1 teaspoon poppy seeds

1 teaspoon salt, or to taste

2 cups vegetable oil or ghee for deep-frying

2 tablespoons vegetable oil or ghee for sautéing

1 clove garlic, chopped

1 Mash the peas and boiled potato together. Add the poppy seeds, red chilies, garam masala, chickpea flour and salt. Mix well to form a thick paste. With this paste form small balls each about the size of a walnut.

2 In a thick-bottomed saucepan or wok, heat the 2 cups of vegetable oil or ghee to smoking point. Turn down the heat and carefully immerse the balls in the hot oil. Fry until balls are a light brown, about 2–3 minutes. (If the cooking temperature is too high, the chickpea flour will not cook thoroughly.) Remove balls with a slotted spoon, letting the excess oil drip back into the pan. Drain further on paper towels.

3 In a thick-bottomed frying pan, heat the vegetable oil or ghee and sauté the onions, garlic and ginger until golden brown. Add the tomatoes, turmeric and 1 teaspoon of coriander; mix well, then add the water and cook for 5 minutes.

A Taste of India
VEGETABLE DISHES

1-inch piece fresh ginger, peeled and chopped fine

2 large onions, chopped fine

1 tomato, chopped fine

1½ teaspoons ground coriander (divided)

½ teaspoon ground turmeric

3 cups water

 Transfer the deep-fried balls to a flat casserole dish and pour sauce over them. Do not stir. Cook 1 more minute over low heat. Then turn off the heat, sprinkle with ½ teaspoon of coriander, and keep covered at low heat in the oven until ready to serve.

Yield: about 7 cups

A Taste of India
VEGETABLE DISHES

Carrot and Pea Curry
(GAAJAR MATAR)

Fast, colorful and delicious!

½ cup vegetable oil or ghee

1 teaspoon oregano (ajwan) seeds

1 large onion, chopped

½ teaspoon crushed dry red chilies

1 tablespoon finely chopped peeled fresh ginger

¼ teaspoon ground turmeric

½ teaspoon salt, or to taste

1 tablespoon tomato paste

¼ teaspoon ground black pepper

2 tablespoons water

2 medium carrots, peeled and cut in ¼-inch slices

½ pound (about 1½ cups) green peas, fresh or frozen

❶ In a large thick-bottomed frying pan or wok, heat the oil or ghee and sauté the onions and ginger until brown. Add the salt, black pepper, oregano seeds, red chilies and turmeric and stir well. Add the tomato paste and 2 tablespoons of water. Stir and cook for 1 minute.

❷ Add the carrots and peas and a cup of water. Cover and cook until the carrots and peas are soft, about 3 minutes. (If using frozen peas, don't add them until the last minute.)

❸ When the water is completely absorbed, continue cooking and stirring the curry until the oil starts to separate out.

Yield: 2½ cups

A Taste of India
VEGETABLE DISHES

Cabbage and Pea Curry
(BAND GOBEE MATAR SABJEE)

Good with plain rice or dahl.

4 tablespoons vegetable oil or ghee

5 cloves garlic, chopped fine

2-inch piece fresh ginger, peeled and chopped fine

1 large onion, chopped

5 green chilies, mild or hot to taste, chopped fine

½ teaspoon salt, or to taste

1 teaspoon crushed dry red chilies

½ small head of cabbage, shredded fine

½ cup water

1 cup (about 5 ounces) green peas, fresh or frozen

1 In a large thick-bottomed frying pan or wok, heat the vegetable oil or ghee and fry the onion, garlic and ginger until light brown. Add green chilies, red chilies and salt and stir for ½ minute.

2 Add the shredded cabbage, peas and water. Cover and cook over low heat until tender, about 5 minutes. Uncover and turn up the heat, frying the mixture until the oil starts to separate out. Stir and serve hot.

Yield: about 2 cups

A Taste of India
VEGETABLE DISHES

Pea and Cheese Curry
(MATAR PANEER)

The very tasty sweet-and-spicy sauce of this dish sets it in a class by itself.

½ pound panir (or tofu)

2 cups vegetable oil or ghee or tofu for deep-frying

2 large onions

¼ teaspoon mustard seeds

6 cloves garlic

1 teaspoon cumin seeds

½ teaspoon ground turmeric

1 teaspoon poppy seeds

½ cup vegetable oil or ghee for frying

2 tablespoons water

2 tablespoons tomato paste (or 2 tomatoes, chopped fine)

3-inch piece fresh ginger, peeled and chopped fine

¼ teaspoon ground nutmeg

❶ Cut the panir (or tofu) into small cubes. In a thick-bottomed saucepan or wok, heat the 2 cups of oil or ghee for deep-frying. Deep-fry the panir or tofu cubes until golden brown. Remove with a slotted spoon, letting the excess oil drip back into the pan. Set aside.

❷ In an electric blender, grind together the onion, garlic, turmeric, mustard seeds, cumin seeds and poppy seeds, making a fine paste without using any water.

❸ In a thick-bottomed frying pan, heat the vegetable oil or ghee and fry this paste, stirring continuously, until brown. Then add the tomato paste (or tomatoes) and 2 tablespoons of water. Keep stirring and cooking until the oil starts to separate out.

❹ Add the ginger, green cardamom seeds, red chilies, nutmeg, bay leaves and salt. Stir thoroughly and add the deep-fried panir (or tofu) cubes. Simmer over low heat for 2 minutes, stirring frequently to prevent sticking.

A Taste of India
VEGETABLE DISHES

2 bay leaves

¼ teaspoon green cardamom seeds

½ teaspoon salt, or to taste

½ teaspoon crushed dry red chilies

1 pint water

½ pound green peas, fresh or frozen (about 1½ cups)

 Add the water and peas and cook over low heat for 10 minutes or until the peas are tender.

Yield: 3 cups

A Taste of India
VEGETABLE DISHES

Melon and Squash Dishes

White Squash Curry
(GHEEAA SABJEE)

Excellent with Lotus Root Kofta Curry (page 104).

3–5 white squash ("patty pan")

3 tablespoons vegetable oil or ghee

1-inch fresh ginger, peeled and chopped fine

2 medium onions, sliced

1 teaspoon oregano (ajwan) seeds

6 cloves garlic, chopped

1 medium tomato, chopped

4 green chilies, mild or hot, to taste, chopped

½ teaspoon ground turmeric

2 bay leaves

1 Peel the squash and cut into small pieces.

2 In a large thick-bottomed frying pan, heat the vegetable oil or ghee and sauté the onions, garlic and ginger and oregano seeds until light brown.

3 Add the tomato and stir well. Next, add the turmeric, bay leaves, red chilies, green chilies and salt, stir thoroughly, and cook until the oil starts to separate out, about 2 minutes.

A Taste of India
VEGETABLE DISHES

½ teaspoon salt, or to taste

½ teaspoon crushed dry red chilies

1 cup water

1 teaspoon garam masala

 Add the chopped squash, stir and add water. Cover and simmer until the squash is tender and all the water is absorbed, about 3–4 minutes. Cook for a short while longer and sprinkle with garam masala before serving.

Yield: 2–3½ cups

A Taste of India
VEGETABLE DISHES

Pumpkin Bhartha: Sweet and Sour
(KHATAA PETHAA)

The exotic sweet-and-spicy flavor of this dish is well complemented by a bland or salty dish.

2 tablespoons tamarind concentrate (or 2 tablespoons mango powder)

½ cup warm water

1 pound pumpkin

2 tablespoons vegetable oil or ghee

1 tablespoon peeled, chopped fresh ginger

2 large onions, chopped

¼ teaspoon ground turmeric

1½ cups water

½ teaspoon mustard seeds

6 green chilies, mild or hot, to taste, chopped fine

1/8 cup honey

1 tablespoon chopped fresh coriander leaves (cilantro)

1. Soak the tamarind or mango powder in ½ cup warm water and set aside.

2. Peel the pumpkin and cut into small pieces.

3. In a thick-bottomed saucepan or wok, heat the oil or ghee, add the onions and ginger and fry until brown. Add the turmeric, mustard seeds and green chilies and stir well. Add the pumpkin pieces, continuing to stir. Add 1½ cups of water and cook until the pumpkin is tender (add more water if necessary to avoid scorching), about 3–4 minutes.

4. Add the tamarind water (step 1) and the honey to the cooking pumpkin mixture. Keep cooking, stirring frequently, until all the water is evaporated and the oil starts to separate out. Garnish with chopped coriander leaves.

Yield: 2½ cups

A Taste of India
VEGETABLE DISHES

Bitter Melon with Yogurt
(KARELAA DAHEE)

A rare treat!

- 4-6 medium-sized bitter melons
- salt for sprinkling on melon
- ½ cup vegetable oil or ghee for frying
- 1 tablespoon finely chopped garlic
- 3 large onions, chopped coarsely
- 1 tablespoon finely chopped peeled fresh ginger
- 1 teaspoon ground cumin
- ½ teaspoon salt, or to taste
- 1 teaspoon ground coriander
- 1 cup yogurt
- 1 teaspoon ground turmeric
- ½ teaspoon crushed dry red chilies

1. Without peeling the bitter melons, cut them into thin slices. Sprinkle with salt and mix well. *Let sit in a bowl for half an hour*, then wash thoroughly and squeeze out the water with your hands. Let them sit for 5 minutes to allow any excess water to drain off. Set aside.

2. In a thick-bottomed frying pan, heat ¼ of the vegetable oil or ghee and fry the chopped onions, garlic and ginger until light brown. Add the cumin, coriander, turmeric and crushed dry red chilies, salt and yogurt, stirring continuously. When the oil starts to separate out from the mixture, remove from the heat.

3. In a separate frying pan, fry the bitter melon in the remaining vegetable oil or ghee until light brown. Next, add it to the onion/yogurt mixture and simmer for a few more minutes.

Yield: 3 cups

A Taste of India
VEGETABLE DISHES

Bitter Melon and Onions
(KARELAA PIAAZ)

2–3 medium-sized bitter melons

salt for sprinkling on bitter melons

2 cups vegetable oil or ghee for deep-frying

6 small onions

1 tablespoon mango powder

1 teaspoon chili powder, mild or spicy, to taste

½ teaspoon salt

① Scrape and peel the bitter melons and cut into small pieces. Place in a bowl, sprinkle with salt and mix well. *Let sit for 1 hour.* Then wash the bitter melon thoroughly and squeeze out the water with your hands. Let sit in the bowl 5 minutes more so any excess water can drain off.

② In a large thick-bottomed saucepan, heat the oil or ghee and deep-fry the bitter melon pieces over medium heat. Keep stirring to make sure the bitter melon fries evenly to a golden brown. Remove with a slotted spoon, letting the excess oil drip back into the pan. Set aside.

③ Chop the onions into quarters. Deep-fry in the same oil until light brown. Remove from the oil with a slotted spoon, letting the excess oil drip back into the pan.

④ In a bowl, mix together the bitter melon and the onions, add the chili powder, mango powder and salt, stir well and serve.

Yield: 3 cups

A Taste of India
VEGETABLE DISHES

Vegetable Koftas in Sauce

Koftas are deep-fried vegetable balls. Easy to make, they are a deliciously different way of preparing vegetables.

Lotus Root Kofta Curry

Lotus root makes this dish enchantingly sweet.

2 pounds lotus root

1 teaspoon oregano (ajwan) seeds

¾ cup chickpea (garbanzo)

8 green chilies, mild or hot, to taste, chopped

1 teaspoon salt, or to taste

½ teaspoon baking soda

2 cups vegetable oil or ghee for deep-frying

1 teaspoon red chili powder

2 teaspoons garam masala

¼ cup vegetable oil or ghee for sautéing

8 cloves garlic, chopped

 If the lotus root is dry, soak it *overnight*.

 Scrape and wash the lotus root and cut into small pieces. Wash again thoroughly. In an electric blender, blend the lotus root with enough water to form a smooth paste. Add the chickpea flour, salt, baking soda, red chili, garam masala, oregano seeds and green chilies. Mix until a thick paste is formed. Use this paste to form small balls each about the size of a walnut, squeezing out excess water as you form them to help them adhere.

 In a thick-bottomed saucepan or wok, heat the 2 cups of vegetable oil or ghee. Deep-fry the lotus root balls over medium heat until light brown. Remove with a slotted spoon, letting the excess oil drip back on the pan, and set aside.

 In a thick-bottomed frying pan, heat the ¼ cup vegetable oil or ghee and sauté the onions, garlic and ginger until brown. Add the tomatoes, cumin, turmeric and 2 teaspoons of coriander. Fry for 2 minutes, add the yogurt and simmer 5 more minutes.

A Taste of India
VEGETABLE DISHES

½ cup finely chopped peeled fresh ginger

4 large onions, chopped

2 large tomatoes, chopped

2 teaspoons ground coriander

1 teaspoon ground cumin

½ cup yogurt

2 teaspoons ground turmeric

2 cups water

½ teaspoon ground coriander

 Add 2 cups of water, turn up the heat, and boil 5 minutes. Turn heat to low, add the koftas and simmer for 2 minutes. Before serving, sprinkle with ½ teaspoon of coriander.

Yield: 48 balls in 3½ cups sauce

A Taste of India
VEGETABLE DISHES

Golden Flower Koftas
(NARGAASEE KOFTAA SABJEE)

This is a fancy party main dish that is good served with plain rice and dahl. *Nargaasee* is the Indian name for the narcissus flower. This dish is named for that flower because the colorful gold-and-white balls, cut in half and arranged on a platter, resemble that flower in bloom.

For the koftas:

1 pound lotus root (4- to 6-inch-long roots) or 2 medium potatoes

2 green chilies, mild or hot, to taste, chopped

6 almonds, soaked, peeled and crushed

2 tablespoons chickpea (garbanzo) flour

panir from 2 quarts of milk, (about 1½ pounds mashed panir)

½ teaspoon garam masala

1 teaspoon ground cumin

1 teaspoon chopped fresh coriander leaves (cilantro)

To make the koftas:

① If using lotus root: Dry lotus root must be soaked in water *overnight*. Peel and cut the lotus root into small pieces. Soak in salted water. Then wash thoroughly and boil or steam until tender. Drain off the water and mash.

If using potatoes: Boil or steam the potatoes until tender. Remove from the water, peel and mash.

② To the mashed vegetables, add the green chilies, chickpea flour, garam masala, cumin, coriander leaves and crushed almonds. Add ¼ of the mashed panir. Mix well and add turmeric to color the mixture yellow.

③ With this mixture, make small balls each the size of a walnut. Cover these balls with a layer of the uncolored panir and form into egg shapes. Then cover these "eggs" with another layer of the yellow mixture.

A Taste of India
VEGETABLE DISHES

4 teaspoons ground turmeric for coloring

2 cups vegetable oil or ghee for deep-frying

For the curry:

3 teaspoons vegetable oil or ghee for sautéing

½ teaspoon garam masala

2 tomatoes, chopped

1 cup chopped onions

6 green cardamom pods (use only the seeds)

6 cloves garlic, chopped

2 teaspoons fresh ginger, peeled and finely chopped

½ teaspoon salt, or to taste

4 cups water

1 teaspoon crushed dry red chilies

 In a thick-bottomed saucepan, heat the 2 cups of vegetable oil or ghee and carefully immerse the "eggs" into the hot oil, deep-frying until brown. Remove with a slotted spoon, letting the excess oil drip back into the pan. Drain further on paper towels.

For the curry sauce:

 In a thick-bottomed frying pan or wok, heat the 3 teaspoons of oil or ghee and sauté the onions until transparent. Add the garlic, ginger and 1 cup of water. Cook until the water is completely evaporated.

 Add the red chilies, garam masala, tomatoes, green cardamom and salt. Continue to cook, stirring continuously, until the oil starts to separate out. Add 3 cups of water and cook until it becomes a soupy gravy, about 15 to 20 minutes.

To serve:

Cut each "egg" in half the long way. Arrange on a platter and pour the curry sauce over them.

Yield: 8–10 "eggs" and 1 cup sauce

A Taste of India
VEGETABLE DISHES

Lotus Root Koftas with Mushrooms
(KANWAL KAKREE EE KHUMBAA)

Really delicious, with a meaty texture!

For the koftas:

1 pound lotus root (4 or 5 six-inch-long roots)

¼ teaspoon ground black cardamom

½ teaspoon ground white cumin

1 teaspoon ground cinnamon

2 teaspoons vegetable oil or ghee for frying

8 teaspoons chickpea (garbanzo) flour

1 teaspoon finely chopped peeled fresh ginger

½ teaspoon garam masala

1 teaspoon cumin seeds

4 green cardamom pods (use only the seeds)

1 teaspoon chopped fresh coriander

1 teaspoon red chili powder

½ teaspoon salt, or to taste

To make the koftas:

① If the lotus root is dry, soak in water *overnight*.

② Peel the lotus root and cut into small pieces. Soak these in salted water for 15 minutes, then drain off the water and wash thoroughly. Boil the lotus root in water with the ground white cumin, black cardamom and cinnamon. When the lotus root is tender, strain off the liquid and mash the lotus root. Set aside.

③ In a thick-bottomed frying pan, heat the 2 tablespoons of vegetable oil or ghee and fry the chickpea flour until light brown. Remove immediately from the heat.

④ To the mashed lotus root add 1 teaspoon ginger, seeds of 4 green cardamom pods, 1 teaspoon cumin seeds, 1 teaspoon coriander leaves, ½ teaspoon salt and the fried flour. Blend it all together until it forms a thick paste.

⑤ With this paste, form small balls each about the size of a walnut. With your thumb, make an indentation in each ball. Finely chop a few of the mushrooms and fill each indentation with them, sealing each with some more lotus root paste. (Set the remaining mushrooms aside for use later.) Roll the balls in the unbleached white flour.

A Taste of India
VEGETABLE DISHES

1 pound mushrooms (about 36 medium-sized)

¼ cup unbleached white flour for dusting

2 cups vegetable oil or ghee for deep-frying

For the curry sauce:

2 teaspoons vegetable oil

36 medium-sized

8 cloves garlic, chopped

2 teaspoons finely chopped peeled fresh ginger

1 cup onions, chopped

1 cup water

½ teaspoon white cumin seeds

¼ teaspoon crushed dry red chilies

½ teaspoon garam masala

1 tomato, peeled and chopped

¼ teaspoon salt, or to taste

½ cup yogurt

3 green cardamom pods (use only the seeds)

2 tablespoons chopped coriander leaves (cilantro)

6 In a thick-bottomed saucepan or wok, heat the 2 cups of oil or ghee and deep-fry the balls over low heat until light brown. Remove with a slotted spoon, letting the excess oil drip back into the pan. Set aside.

To make the curry sauce:

1 In a large thick-bottomed frying pan, heat the 2 teaspoons of vegetable oil or ghee and sauté the onions, garlic and 2 teaspoons of ginger until light brown. Add 1 cup of water, ¼ teaspoon red chilies, tomatoes, seeds of 3 cardamom pods, cumin seeds, 1/3 teaspoon of garam masala, ¼ teaspoon salt and yogurt. Stir continuously and cook until all the liquid is absorbed and the oil starts to separate out. Add the remaining mushrooms, stirring frequently to prevent sticking. Cook until the mushrooms are done.

2 Ten minutes before serving, add the deep-fried balls to the curry and cook over low heat, stirring very gently, until the curry has saturated the balls. Sprinkle with 2 tablespoons of coriander leaves before serving.

Yield: 12 balls and 2½ cups sauce

A Taste of India
VEGETABLE DISHES

Deep-Fried Panir in Curry Sauce
(PANEER KOFTAA KAREE)

Serve with plain rice and a sweet chutney.

2 tablespoons unbleached white flour

enough water to make a thin batter

¼ teaspoon salt, or to taste

1 cup panir, cut into cubes

2 cups vegetable oil or ghee for deep-frying

¼ cup vegetable oil or ghee for sautéing

1 tablespoon finely chopped peeled fresh ginger

2 medium onions, chopped

4 green chilies, mild or hot, to taste, chopped

6 cloves garlic, chopped

½ teaspoon red chili powder

1. In a bowl, sift together the flour and ¼ teaspoon of salt and add enough water to make a thin batter.

2. Dip the panir cubes in the batter.

3. In a thick-bottomed saucepan, heat the 2 cups of vegetable oil or ghee and deep-fry the coated panir cubes until light brown. Remove with a slotted spoon, letting the excess oil drip back into the pan. Drain further on paper towels.

4. In a large thick-bottomed frying pan or wok, heat the ¼ cup of vegetable oil or ghee and sauté the onions, garlic, ginger and green chilies until golden brown. Add the red chili powder, turmeric, salt, cumin, poppy seeds, cloves, green cardamom and almonds. Stir well, add 2 tablespoons of water, and sauté until the oil starts to separate out.

A Taste of India
VEGETABLE DISHES

4 green cardamom pods (use only the seeds)

1 teaspoon ground turmeric

½ teaspoon salt, or to taste

12 almonds, peeled* and chopped fine

1 teaspoon ground cumin

1 teaspoon poppy seeds

2 tablespoons water

4 whole cloves

½ cup yogurt

enough water to make sauce

1 tablespoon chopped fresh coriander (cilantro) or mint leaves

5 Add the yogurt and simmer for a few minutes, stirring continuously. Add enough water to make a soupy sauce and cook 5 more minutes.

6 Add the deep-fried panir. Continue cooking over low heat for 5 minutes. Remove from the heat, sprinkle with chopped coriander or mint leaves and serve.

Yield: 16 cubes panir and 4 cups sauce

* Peel the almonds by immersing in boiling water for a few minutes; the skins can then be "pinched" off.

A Taste of India
VEGETABLE DISHES

Banana Kofta Curry
(KELAA KOFTAA)

An excellent dish with a most unusual taste.

For the koftas:

4 unripe bananas

1-inch piece fresh ginger, peeled and chopped fine

½ teaspoon salt, or to taste

juice of 1 lemon

1 medium onion, finely chopped

3 tablespoons grated mild cheese, such as cheddar

2 cups vegetable oil or ghee for deep-frying

For the curry sauce:

¼ vegetable oil or ghee

6 cloves garlic, chopped

1 teaspoon finely chopped peeled fresh ginger

2 medium onions, chopped

To make the koftas:

1. Peel the bananas, steam until soft and mash.

2. In a blender grind the ginger and onions together. Transfer to a bowl and add the salt, lemon juice, grated cheese and mashed bananas. Mix thoroughly to form a thick paste.

3. Form this mixture into small balls each about the size of a walnut. In a thick-bottomed saucepan or wok, heat the 2 cups of oil or ghee and deep-fry the banana balls over medium heat until golden brown. Remove with a slotted spoon, letting the excess oil drip back into the pan. Set aside.

To make the curry:

1. In a large thick-bottomed frying pan, heat the vegetable oil or ghee and sauté the onions, garlic and ginger until golden brown.

2. Add the tomatoes, green chilies, turmeric, red chili powder and salt. Mix well and simmer for a few minutes. When the tomatoes soften and the oil starts to separate out, add enough water to make a sauce. Boil for 5 minutes.

A Taste of India
VEGETABLE DISHES

2 medium tomatoes, chopped

½ teaspoon red chili powder

4 green chilies, mild or hot, to taste, chopped fine

½ teaspoon salt, or to taste

enough water to make a sauce

1 teaspoon ground turmeric

1 cup cream

For the garnish:

a few fresh coriander leaves (cilantro)

1 pinch of garam masala

3 Turn off the heat. In a bowl, beat the cream a little to thicken it but not till it foams, then add to curry sauce, mixing well. Place the banana balls in a flat casserole. Pour the sauce over the balls but do not stir. Place the casserole, covered, in a warm oven until ready to serve. Before serving, garnish with fresh coriander leaves and a sprinkle of garam masala.

Yield: 5–6 cups

A Taste of India
VEGETABLE DISHES

Stuffed Vegetables

❦

Stuffed Potato Bhujia

The sauce makes this fancy party dish taste just divine!

For the potatos:

3 medium potatoes

3 teaspoons butter or ghee

¼ teaspoon salt, or to taste

For the filling:

1 cup panir

2 tablespoons raisins

a few fresh coriander leaves (cilantro)

1 green chili, mild or hot, to taste, chopped

½ teaspoon salt, or to taste

2 tablespoons tomato sauce

1 tablespoon ground cumin

1 tablespoon finely chopped peeled fresh ginger

① Bake the potatoes until tender. Cut them in half and scoop out the insides. Mash the potato pulp with ¼ teaspoon salt and 3 teaspoons butter or ghee and set aside.

② In a bowl, mix together all of the filling ingredients.

③ Half-fill the hollow potatoes with the filling mixture, then finish filling with the mashed potatoes. Lightly dust the filled potatoes with flour. Oil a baking pan with 4 tablespoons oil or ghee. Place potatoes on pan and bake at 350 degrees till warmed through, 10–15 minutes.

④ While the potatoes are in the oven, heat ½ tablespoon of ghee in a small pan. Add ½ tablespoon white flour, ½ teaspoon of asafoetida and the yogurt. Add the 2 teaspoons of cumin, garam masala, 1 teaspoon ginger, red chili powder and a few coriander leaves. Sauté for a few minutes. Add ¼ teaspoon of salt and chopped tomatoes and continue to cook for a few minutes.

A Taste of India
VEGETABLE DISHES

unbleached flour for dusting

4 tablespoons vegetable oil or ghee

potatoes

½ tablespoon ghee

½ teaspoon asafoetida

½ tablespoon white flour

1½ cups yogurt

2 teaspoons ground cumin

¾ teaspoons red chili powder, mild or hot, to taste

1 teaspoon garam masala

1 teaspoon ground ginger

a few, fresh coriander leaves (cilantro)

¼ teaspoon salt, or to taste

1 tomato, chopped

Garnish:

a few more coriander leaves (cilantro)

 Pour sauce over the potatoes and garnish with coriander leaves.

Yield: 6 stuffed potato halves

A Taste of India
VEGETABLE DISHES

Stuffed Bell Peppers
(SIMLAA MIRACH BUJIAA)

6 medium bell peppers (sweet green peppers)

4 medium potatoes

salted water for boiling

½ pound (about 1½ cups) potatoes and peas green peas, fresh or frozen

3 tablespoons vegetable oil or ghee for frying

1 teaspoon finely chopped peeled fresh ginger

1 white onion, chopped fine

¼ teaspoon ground turmeric

½ teaspoon salt, or to taste

¼ teaspoon red chili powder

¼ teaspoon pomegranate seeds

¼ teaspoon mango powder

½ teaspoon garam masala

4 tablespoons vegetable oil or ghee for baking

1. Wash the bell peppers and immerse in boiling water for 1 minute. They will become crisper and lighter in color. Carefully remove from the water, drain and cool.

2. Peel the potatoes and cut into small cubes. Boil the potatoes and peas together in salted water, using as little water as possible. When they are cooked, drain off any leftover water and mash the vegetables together.

3. In a large thick-bottomed frying pan, heat 3 tablespoons of vegetable oil or ghee and fry the onions and ginger until golden brown. Add the turmeric, chili powder, mango powder, garam masala, ½ teaspoon salt and pomegranate seeds, and mix well. Add the mashed vegetables, stir thoroughly, and fry for a few more minutes. Remove from the heat.

4. Carefully cut the stems off the peppers and scoop out the seeds. Stuff each pepper with the vegetable mixture. Tie twine around each pepper so the stuffing cannot fall out during cooking.

5. Oil a baking pan with 4 tablespoons oil or ghee and place the peppers on it. Bake the peppers at 350 degrees until they begin to brown, about 40 minutes. Remove from the oven, snip off the twine and serve.

Yield: 6 stuffed peppers

A Taste of India
VEGETABLE DISHES

Stuffed Bitter Melon
(KARELAA MASAALEWAALAA)

2-3 medium-sized bitter melons

a pinch or two of salt to sprinkle on melons

2 tablespoons pomegranate seeds or mango powder

1 teaspoon ground turmeric

1 teaspoon garam masala

3 medium onions, wchopped very fine

1 teaspoon salt, or to taste

¼ cup vegetable oil or ghee for frying (optional)

1 teaspoon red chili powder

3 tablespoons vegetable oil or ghee for baking

1. To prepare the bitter melons: Peel and scrape the bitter melons and cut lengthwise. Remove the seeds. Sprinkle the melons with salt, place in a bowl, and set aside for 1 hour. Then thoroughly wash the melons so that the salt and bitterness is washed out. Squeeze them gently with your hands to remove all excess liquid.

2. Grind the pomegranate seeds and mix with the onions, chili powder, turmeric, garam masala and salt. (Optional: sauté these ingredients in vegetable oil or ghee before continuing with step 3.)

3. Stuff the bitter melons with this mixture. Tie the melons with twine so the stuffing cannot fall out during cooking.

4. Oil a baking pan with 3 tablespoons oil or ghee and place melons on it. Bake the melons at 350 degrees until they begin to brown, about 40 minutes. Remove from the oven, snip off the twine and serve.

Yield: 2 or 3 stuffed melons

A Taste of India
VEGETABLE DISHES

Stuffed Cabbage
(MASAALEWAALEE BAND GOBEE)

This is a lightly spiced, satisfying side dish for special occasions.

1 large cabbage

salted water for blanching

24 large potatoes

¼ cup vegetable oil or ghee

2 large green chilies, mild or hot, to taste, chopped fine

2 large onions, chopped

4 cloves garlic, chopped

1 bunch fresh coriander leaves (cilantro)

1-inch piece fresh ginger, peeled and chopped fine

½ teaspoon chili powder, or to taste

1 teaspoon ground turmeric

1. To prepare the cabbage leaves for rolling: In boiling salted water, blanch the cabbage leaves, 2 at a time, for 4-5 minutes, until leaves but not stems soften, but not till leaves change color. Remove from the water, drain, cover with a towel to prevent drying, and set aside to cool.

2. While you are blanching batches of leaves, boil the potatoes until tender, peel and cut into small pieces.

3. In a large thick-bottomed frying pan or wok, heat the oil or ghee and sauté the onions, garlic, ginger, green chilies, and coriander leaves until the onions are golden brown.

4. Add the chili powder, garam masala, turmeric, salt and the potatoes. Sauté for 3 minutes, stirring frequently.

5. Remove from the heat, sprinkle with lemon juice, mix well, and set aside to cool.

A Taste of India
VEGETABLE DISHES

½ teaspoon salt, or to taste

½ teaspoon garam masala

juice of 1 lemon

 Remove the hard stems from the blanched cabbage leaves and spread the leaves out on a flat surface. Put a portion of the potato mixture at the edge of each cabbage leaf, gently turn the sides of the leaf inward and roll up the mixture in the leaf. (If the leaves are small, lay 2 leaves overlapping each other and roll as one.) Serve hot.

Yield: 15–20 stuffed leaves

Tofu Dishes

Long a staple in the diet of people in Japan and China, in recent years, tofu has become very popular in India, because of its many health benefits, as well as its wonderful versatility. Its chameleon-like qualities give tofu the ability to absorb flavors through spices and marinades and adapt to a vast variety of tastes and textures in delicious and fulfilling dishes.

Tofu is naturally high in protein, calcium, and vitamin E, and low in fat. There is a common misconception that vegetarians cannot get as much protein as those who consume meat. Although vegetables are mainly composed of carbohydrates, some vegetables and legumes, especially in combination with a grain—such as rice or quinoa—render all of the essential amino acids that your body requires; and proteins from vegetables and legumes are more easily absorbed by the body. Tofu is a unique and excellent form of vegetable protein, in that it is a complete protein on its own, with all of the essential amino acids present.

In the West, we are seeing that the health benefits claimed by the Asian world are born out in study after study. Tofu has been gaining in popularity in the West among vegetarians, including vegans, over the past several decades. Consuming tofu regularly is shown to help lower bad cholesterol, reduce the risk of cardiovascular diseases, alleviate symptoms associated with menopause, lower the risk of cancer, and help make bones stronger in middle age, helping to prevent osteoporosis. In addition, tofu is an antioxidant that neutralizes free radicals, slowing the aging process.

Widely available in most markets, tofu is made from soybeans, water and a coagulant, or curdling agent, hence it is sometimes called bean curd. You can look for tofu in the refrigerated section of your grocery store. When cooking with tofu, you will usually want to drain and press the tofu first.

Enjoy this sampling of tofu recipes from some of my favorite tofu dishes.

A Taste of India
VEGETABLE DISHES

Baked Tofu

1 container tofu

1 tablespoon oil or ghee

1 teaspoon ground turmeric

½ teaspoon salt

1 tablespoon crushed dry chilies

Preheat oven to 350 degrees.

① Cut tofu into 8 slices. Transfer to a baking tray and bake for 10 minutes. Remove the baked pieces from the oven.

② Mix together oil or ghee, turmeric, salt and chilies. Spread this mixture evenly over the tofu pieces.

③ Bake for 10 minutes longer, flipping the pieces halfway through. When tofu is a light golden brown, it is done. Let cool slightly and serve.

Yield: 8 pieces

A Taste of India
VEGETABLE DISHES

BBQ Tofu Ribs

Baking Marinade Sauce:

4 tablespoons peanut butter

2 tablespoons tamari

½ teaspoon garlic powder

pinch of black pepper

1/3 cup water

Barbeque Sauce:

1 tablespoons molasses

1 teaspoon prepared yellow mustard

½ teaspoon garlic powder

½ teaspoon onion powder

1 tablespoon honey, brown sugar or maple syrup

1 cup ketchup

2 containers tofu, frozen and defrosted, water squeezed out

① In a small bowl, mix together the Baking Marinade Sauce ingredients. Set aside.

② In a small saucepan, combine all the Barbeque Sauce ingredients. Cook over medium heat for 10 minutes.

③ Cut tofu into 8 slabs, approximately 1/2" thick. Place on a well-oiled baking tray. Heat oven to 350 degrees.

④ Pour Baking Marinade Sauce over the tofu. Bake 20 minutes, then turn tofu over and bake 15 minutes more.

⑤ Pour Barbeque Sauce over the "ribs" and bake for 15 minutes.

Yield: 8 pieces

A Taste of India
VEGETABLE DISHES

Curried Tofu with Toasted Nuts

While the tofu bakes, prepare the grain dish that you would like. Rice, quinoa and millet can all prepared in 20 minutes or less.

1 container tofu, frozen and defrosted, water squeezed out

2 tablespoons tamari or Bragg Liquid Aminos

1 tablespoon almond butter

2 teaspoons honey

1 tablespoon curry powder

1 teaspoon onion powder

3 vegetable cubes or 2 teaspoons vegetable powder

3 cups water

3 tablespoons arrowroot or cornstarch

½ cup toasted walnuts (or almonds or nuts of choice)

1 tablespoon chopped green onions

1 tablespoon chopped fresh coriander leaves (cilantro)

Preheat oven to 350 degrees.

1. Cut tofu into pieces approximately 1 inch by ½ inch.

2. In a large bowl, mix together the tamari (or Bragg Liquid Aminos), almond butter, honey, curry powder and onion powder. Add the tofu pieces and mix till pieces are coated thoroughly.

3. Place tofu pieces on an oiled baking sheet or tray and bake for 15 minutes. Turn pieces over and bake 10 more minutes.

4. While tofu is baking, mix in a large saucepan the water, vegetable cubes/powder and arrowroot/cornstarch. Turn heat to low and stir so that a smooth sauce is created.

5. Add the baked tofu to the saucepan and heat thoroughly.

Serve on top of grain, garnished with nuts and chopped green onions and coriander leaves.

Yield: 3 cups

A Taste of India
VEGETABLE DISHES

Chili with Tofu and Beans

¼ cup water

2 tablespoons tamari or Bragg Liquid Aminos

1 tablespoon peanut butter

1 teaspoon onion powder

½ teaspoon cumin seeds

½ teaspoon garlic powder

1 container texturized tofu pieces

¼ cup olive oil

1 large onion, diced

1 large green bell pepper, diced

1 large red bell pepper, diced

2–3 cloves garlic, minced

1 bay leaf

¼ teaspoon coriander seeds

1. In a bowl, mix the water, tamari (or Braggs), peanut butter, onion powder, cumin seeds and garlic powder. Pour over the texturized tofu and let marinate for 15 minutes to a half hour.

2. Heat oven to 350 degrees. Transfer tofu pieces to an oiled baking sheet or cast-iron pan. Bake 20 minutes, then flip pieces over and bake 10 more minutes.

3. While tofu is baking, heat the olive oil in a large, heavy-bottomed soup pot. Add the onion, red and green bell peppers, garlic, bay leaf and coriander seeds, and sauté.

4. When the vegetables are tender, add the cooked pinto beans and water to cover, along with the chili powder, paprika, ground coriander, salt and optional green chilies.

A Taste of India
VEGETABLE DISHES

2½ cups cooked pinto beans

1 tablespoon chili powder

¼ teaspoon paprika

¼ teaspoon ground coriander

1 teaspoon salt, or to taste

¼ cup chopped green chilies, optional

 Add the baked texturized tofu to the pot. Heat thoroughly on high simmer for 10 minutes and serve.

Yield: 1½ quarts

A Taste of India
VEGETABLE DISHES

Mixed Vegetables with Tofu Fried Rice

1 tablespoon olive oil

½ cup shredded carrots (about 2 carrots)

1 cup diced celery

1 medium onion, diced

2 cloves garlic, minced

½ cup broccoli florets

1 zucchini, shredded or diced

2 tablespoons olive oil

1½ containers tofu, diced

1 teaspoon garlic powder 2 tablespoons Bragg Liquid Aminos

juice of ½ a lemon

3–4 cups of cooked brown or white rice

½ cup grated cheese (optional)

½ cup nutritional yeast flakes (optional)

1. Heat the oil in a large skillet and sauté the carrots, celery, onion, and garlic for 10 minutes, until tender.

2. Steam the zucchini and the broccoli for 19 minutes, until tender, separately, and then add to the above vegetables.

3. In a second skillet, heat 2 tablespoons of oil. Add the tofu, garlic powder, Bragg Liquid Aminos and lemon juice. Sauté over medium heat for about 5 minutes, stirring often, until tofu is lightly browned. Set aside.

4. Add the fried tofu and cooked rice to the vegetables, mix well. Heat thoroughly and serve, topped with grated cheese and nutritional yeast flakes if desired.

Yield: 2 quarts

Note:

This dish can be baked instead of fried. In this case you can add more vegetables. Fry the onions with cumin, salt and pepper. Add water to this with vegetable powder or a vegetable cube, then mix in the rice and other vegetables, along with optional cheese and nutritional yeast flakes. Transfer to a baking pan and bake at 350 degrees for 25 minutes, covered and then uncovered for 15 minutes. Serve with lots of fresh cilantro, parsley and any other fresh herbs.

A Taste of India
VEGETABLE DISHES

Pan-Fried Tofu with Nutritional Yeast Flakes

Tofu prepared this way is great for sandwiches.

1 container tofu

1 tablespoon olive oil

2 tablespoons Bragg Liquid Aminos, or to taste

¼ cup nutritional yeast flakes

1 Cut tofu into 8 slices.

2 Add one tablespoon of olive oil to thick-bottomed pan, and lay the sliced tofu in the pan. Brown tofu on both sides over medium heat for about 3 minutes on each side.

3 Sprinkle Bragg Liquid Aminos over the browned tofu. Let cook for 1 minute, then turn over each slice. Add a layer of nutritional yeast flakes over the top side of tofu, according to taste, and cook until golden brown, for about 1 more minute.

Serve warm.

Yield: 8 slices

A Taste of India
VEGETABLE DISHES

Scrambled Tofu

1½ tablespoons vegetable oil or ghee

1 teaspoon cumin seeds

1 large tomato, chopped

½ teaspoon ground turmeric

½ teaspoon crushed dry red chilies, or to taste

½ teaspoon salt, or to taste

1 container soft tofu, crumbled

2 tablespoons finely chopped fresh coriander leaves (cilantro)

① In a medium saucepan, heat the oil or ghee. Add cumin seeds and sauté 2 minutes.

② Add the chopped tomato, turmeric, chilies, and salt. Cook over medium heat, stirring, for 2–3 minutes.

③ Add crumbled tofu. Cook over medium heat about 5 minutes, until no water is left, and the oil starts to separate.

④ Mix in chopped coriander leaves and serve.

Yield: 2 servings

Note: You can add sautéed onions, peeled and chopped fresh ginger, or diced mild green chilies in the beginning to customize your dish.

A Taste of India
VEGETABLE DISHES

Scrambled Tofu and Peas

1 tablespoon olive oil

½ onion, chopped

½ teaspoon cumin seeds

½ teaspoon ground turmeric

¼ teaspoon crushed dry red chilies

2 cups frozen peas

1 container soft tofu, crumbled

Bragg Liquid Aminos to taste, or salt

½ cup chopped nuts

freshly chopped coriander leaves (cilantro)

1 Heat the olive oil in a medium skillet. Add the chopped onions and sauté until lightly browned, about 2 minutes.

2 Add the cumin seeds, turmeric, dry red chilies and peas. Cook 1 minute, then add the tofu. Cook and stir for about 5 minutes, until all liquid has evaporated and the mixture is slightly browned. Add Bragg Liquid Aminos or salt to taste.

Sprinkle with chopped coriander leaves and serve.

Yield: 4 servings

A Taste of India
VEGETABLE DISHES

Scrambled Tofu with Green Chilies

1 tablespoon olive oil

½ teaspoon cumin seeds

3 chopped Roma tomatoes or other medium tomatoes

1 container soft tofu, crumbled

½ teaspoon ground coriander

½ teaspoon ground turmeric

1 tablespoon salt or Bragg Liquid Aminos

6 ounces fresh or canned diced mild green chilies

chopped fresh coriander leaves (cilantro)

1. Heat the olive oil in a medium skillet. Add the cumin seeds and sauté 1 minute over medium heat.

2. Add the chopped tomatoes and cook 3-4 minutes, until tender. Add tofu, ground coriander, turmeric, and salt (or Bragg Liquid Aminos). Cook together for 3 minutes, or until most of the moisture has evaporated, and then add the green chilies. Cook for 3 minutes.

Garnish with chopped fresh coriander leaves and serve.

Yield: 4 servings

A Taste of India
VEGETABLE DISHES

Stuffed Peppers with Tofu and Quinoa

Make the sauce while the peppers are baking.

2 tablespoons olive oil

1 onion, chopped

1 clove garlic

½ cup grated zucchini

½ cup crumbled tofu

½ cup cooked quinoa

1 teaspoon each of chopped fresh basil, parsley, thyme and rosemary

¼ teaspoon salt

pinch of black pepper

4 bell peppers, tops cut off and seeded*

For the sauce:

1 tablespoon olive oil

half an onion, grated

½ teaspoon flour

1 clove garlic, minced

1 cup tomato sauce

¼ cup water

salt and pepper to taste

Preheat oven to 350 degrees.

1 Steam the bell peppers for about 5 minutes and set aside.

2 In a medium skillet, heat the olive oil. Add the onion, garlic and grated zucchini and sauté over medium heat about 4 minutes, until tender.

3 Add the crumbled tofu, cooked quinoa, herbs, salt and pepper. Sauté for 1 minute. Remove from heat.

4 Stuff the peppers with the filling. Transfer to an oiled baking dish. Bake at 350 degrees for 30 minutes or until peppers are tender.

To make the sauce:

1 In a saucepan, heat the olive oil over medium heat. Add the grated onion and flour and cook, stirring, 1 minute. Add the minced garlic, tomato sauce and water. Continue cooking 5 more minutes, stirring occasionally, until thick.

2 Pour over the stuffed baked tomatoes or peppers as they come out the oven.

Yield: 4 stuffed peppers

A Taste of India
VEGETABLE DISHES

Swiss Chard Rolls with Tofu

1 onion, sliced into half-moons

1 tomato, sliced into half-moons

1 container tofu, crumbled

1 tablespoon garlic powder

1 tablespoon onion powder

1 tablespoon tamari or Bragg Liquid Aminos

juice of ½ a lemon

3 tablespoons olive oil

1 tablespoon nutritional yeast flakes

pinch of salt

¼ pound mushrooms (optional), sautéed in a bit of butter

1 head Swiss chard, washed, dried, leaves carefully separated

2 tablespoons chopped toasted walnuts

1 In medium skillet, sauté onions in 1 tablespoon of olive oil for 5 minutes, until tender. Add tomatoes, olive oil, and salt and continue cooking for 3 minutes. Set aside.

2 Sauté tofu in in 1 tablespoon of olive oil, with garlic powder, onion powder, tamari (or Braggs) and lemon juice for about 5 minutes. When the liquid has almost disappeared, add 1 tablespoon each of olive oil and nutritional yeast flakes and stir until all the tofu has been covered. Set aside.

3 In a large pot equipped with a vegetable steamer, lightly steam the kale leaves—they should be tender but not totally limp. Spread the individual leaves wide on a large plate or tray.

4 Preheat oven to 350 degrees. Combine the tofu mixture with the onions and tomatoes (and sautéed mushrooms, if using). Spread a spoonful of the filling onto a chard leaf, then roll up the leaf up into a log-shaped roll. Repeat with remaining leaves and filling. Transfer rolls to an oiled baking pan and bake 30 minutes.

Serve warm with walnuts sprinkled on top, accompanied by the grain of your choice.

Yield: 4 servings

A Taste of India
VEGETABLE DISHES

❦

Tofu Potato Vegetable Casserole

This can be a great meal made from leftovers, or you can start from scratch.

2 cups mashed potatoes

2 cups mashed turnips

1 container tofu, mashed

¼ cup chopped fresh parsley and any other fresh herbs that inspire you

pinch of ground sage

1 teaspoon garlic powder

¼ teaspoon black pepper

1¼ teaspoons salt

1 onion, chopped

2 tablespoons olive oil or ghee

1 carrot, finely chopped

half a head of broccoli, cut into small florets (about ¼ cup)

1 zucchini, diced

Preheat oven to 350 degrees.

① In a large bowl, mix together the potatoes, turnips, tofu and all the spices and herbs. Set aside.

② Steam the carrots and broccoli florets until tender, about 10 minutes.

③ In a skillet, sauté onions in olive oil until translucent and tender, about 5 minutes.

④ In an oiled baking, combine all ingredients and bake for 20 minutes at 350 degrees. Enjoy.

Yield: 6 servings

A Taste of India
VEGETABLE DISHES

Tofu Vegetable Stir-Fry with Coconut

1 onion, cut into half-moon slices

1-inch piece of fresh ginger, peeled and chopped into thin matchsticks

2 cloves garlic, minced

1 tablespoon nutritional yeast flakes

1 teaspoon garlic powder

1 container tofu, cut into ½-inch cubes

4 tablespoons sesame oil

2 carrots, thinly sliced like coins

1 head of broccoli, chopped into bite-size pieces

1 red bell pepper, sliced

1 cup chopped mushrooms

① *Smash the root of the lemon grass and let soak it in the coconut milk for 10-15 minutes.*

② Sauté the onions in 2 tablespoons of sesame oil about 5 minutes or until tender. Add the ginger and pieces of the tender part of the lemon grass and cook 3 minutes. Add the garlic and cook until softened, about 2 minutes. Set aside.

③ In a bowl mix the nutritional yeast flakes and garlic powder. Add the tofu and coat it with this mixture.

④ Heat 2 tablespoons of sesame oil in a skillet and sauté the coated tofu over medium high heat until slightly crispy. Set aside.

⑤ Steam the carrots, broccoli, bell pepper, and mushrooms about 5 minutes, or until tender.

⑥ In a large skillet combine the cooked tofu, steamed vegetables, bean sprouts and green onions. Pour in the coconut milk, tamari, and red chilies, if using. Heat thoroughly on medium heat for 5 minutes or until milk is simmering and slightly thickened. Sprinkle tamari and mix well.

A Taste of India
VEGETABLE DISHES

½ cup snow peas (optional)

½ cup bean sprouts

½ cup chopped green onions

1 cup coconut milk

¼ cup tamari

1 stalk of fresh lemon grass

pinch of crushed dry red chilies (optional)

chopped fresh coriander leaves (cilantro)

Serve hot, topped with coriander leaves, with a side of steamed rice.

Yield: 4 servings

YOGURT DISHES, SOUPS AND SALADS

Yogurt dishes (raita) are an essential part of an Indian meal. Their coolness, smooth texture, white color and relatively mild taste serve as a refreshing oasis amid the many colorful, flavor-rich dishes.

When choosing which raita to serve with a meal, be sure to pick one that complements the main dish; a cool, fruit or mint raita goes well with a spicy vegetable while a raita with vegetables and onions balances a quieter rice or bean dish. Thick, rich, creamy yogurt makes the best raita.

Traditionally, soup and salad are not found in Indian cuisine, but with the free flow of East-West culture, modern India has created many wonderful soups and salads that have a distinctive Indian flair.

Cream of Almond Soup is very light in taste. For other light soups, you'll find that most dahl (bean) dishes, thinned out with a little extra water and liquefied in a food processor, can also serve as a soup course.

The salads can either start the meal, be served right along with the other main dishes the way raita is, or be offered as light meals in themselves.

Yogurt Dishes—Raita

Cucumber Yogurt
(KHEERAA RAAITAA)

2 cups yogurt

1 tablespoon fresh coriander leaves (cilantro), chopped

1 cup cucumber, peeled and grated

¼ teaspoon ground nutmeg

1 teaspoon ground cumin

½ teaspoon salt, or to taste

½ teaspoon ground black pepper

In a bowl, beat the yogurt with a whisk or an egg beater until it is creamy. Add the remaining ingredients and mix well. Chill 30 minutes before serving.

Yield: 2½ cups

A Taste of India
YOGURT DISHES, SOUPS AND SALADS

Baked Eggplant Yogurt
(BAIGAN RAAITAA)

1 small eggplant

1 teaspoon ground black pepper

vegetable oil to coat eggplant

½ teaspoon salt, or to taste

2 cups yogurt

Garnish:

1 teaspoon ground cumin

¼ teaspoon ground nutmeg

Preheat the oven to 350 degrees.

1 Wash the eggplant, dry it off, oil the skin, and pierce it a few times with a knife. Place on a rack in the middle of the oven and bake until very soft, 30-40 minutes.

2 Remove eggplant from the oven and let cool. Peel off the skin, place the pulp in a bowl and mash until smooth. Add the yogurt and mix well. Stir in the pepper and salt. Garnish with a sprinkling of ground cumin and nutmeg.

Yield: 2½ cups

A Taste of India
YOGURT DISHES, SOUPS AND SALADSS

Festival Yogurt

(AALOO, PIAAZ, TAMAATAR, POODEENAA RAAITAA)

2 cups yogurt

1 small bunch mint leaves, chopped fine

1 medium onion, chopped fine

1 teaspoon ground black pepper

1 large tomato, chopped fine

1 medium potato, boiled, peeled and diced

1 teaspoon cumin seeds, roasted and ground

½ teaspoon salt, or to taste

Garnish:

a pinch of ground cumin

In a bowl, beat the yogurt with a whisk or an egg beater until it is creamy. Add the onion, tomato, potato, mint, black pepper, cumin and salt and mix well. Garnish with a sprinkle of cumin powder.

Yield: 3½ cups

A Taste of India
YOGURT DISHES, SOUPS AND SALADS

Banana Yogurt
(KELE RAAITAA)

Peppery sweet-and-sour in taste, this raita is great with a bland rice dish.

2 cups yogurt

2 tablespoons raisins, (soaked in for 10 minutes, then water drained)

½ teaspoon ground black pepper

1 tablespoon honey

½ teaspoon lemon juice

2 large bananas, peeled and sliced thin

¼ teaspoon salt, or to taste

In a bowl, beat the yogurt with a whisk or an egg beater until it is creamy. Mix in the black pepper, honey, lemon juice, salt and raisins. Add the bananas and stir well, being careful not to mash them. Chill 30 minutes before serving.

Yield: about 2½ cups

A Taste of India
YOGURT DISHES, SOUPS AND SALADSS

Spiced Potato Yogurt
(AALOO RAAITAA)

For a light meal, serve this raita with vegetables. If you prefer less spice, omit the chili powder.

1 cup yogurt

½ teaspoon salt, or to taste

½ teaspoon ground black pepper

½ cup thinly sliced boiled potatoes

¼ teaspoon red chili powder

1-2 splashes milk, if necessary

½ teaspoon cumin seeds, roasted and ground

Garnish:

1 teaspoon chopped fresh coriander leaves (cilantro)

In a bowl, beat the yogurt with a whisk or an egg beater until it is creamy. Add the black pepper, red chili powder, cumin and salt and mix well. Add the potatoes and gently mix so that they are all covered with yogurt. Add a splash or two of milk if needed to thin the yogurt so that it covers the potatoes adequately. Garnish with coriander leaves. Chill for 3–4 hours before serving.

Yield: 1½ cups

A Taste of India

YOGURT DISHES, SOUPS AND SALADS

Mint Yogurt

(POODEENAA RAAITAA)

½ cup finely chopped fresh mint leaves

3 tablespoons grated fresh coconut

½ cup chopped fresh coriander leaves (cilantro)

6 green chilies, mild or hot, to taste, chopped

2 cups yogurt

¼ teaspoon ground nutmeg (optional)

½ teaspoon salt, or to taste

1. In an electric blender, blend together the mint leaves, coriander leaves, coconut, green chilies, and just enough water to moisten the mixture (¼ cup or less).

2. In a bowl, beat the yogurt with a whisk or an egg beater until it is creamy. Add the blended ingredients, along with the salt and nutmeg, and mix well. Serve chilled.

Yield: 2½–3 cups

A Taste of India
YOGURT DISHES, SOUPS AND SALADSS

Mint Chutney Yogurt
(POODEENAA CHATNEE RAAITAA)

1 cup fresh mint leave

2 tablespoons lemon juice or 1 tablespoon tamarind concentrate (seedless)

2 tablespoons finely chopped peeled fresh ginger

1 small onion, quartered

1 teaspoon cumin seeds

2–4 green chilies, mild or hot, to taste

2 cups yogurt

2 teaspoons honey (optional)

ground black pepper (garnish)

① In an electric blender, blend together the mint leaves, ginger, onion, green chilies, cumin seeds and lemon juice or tamarind concentrate with just enough water to moisten the mixture (¼ cup or less).

② In a bowl, beat the yogurt with a whisk or an egg beater until it is creamy. Add the blended ingredients and mix well. Garnish with a little black pepper sprinkled on top.

Yield: 3 cups

Note: If you want to make this raita sweet-and-sour, stir in 2 teaspoons of honey.

A Taste of India
YOGURT DISHES, SOUPS AND SALADS

Peanut and Raisin Yogurt
(MOONGPHALEE RAAITAA)

This raita has an exotic texture and taste.

½ cup shelled roasted peanuts

½ teaspoon ground black pepper

2 cups yogurt

½ teaspoon red chili powder

¼ cup raisins, soaked in water for 10 minutes, then drained)

¼ teaspoon salt, or to taste

1 tablespoon honey

Garnish:

½ teaspoon ground cumin

 In an electric blender or coffee grinder, grind the peanuts to the consistency of meal.

 In a bowl, beat the yogurt with a whisk or an egg beater until it is creamy. Add the ground peanuts, raisins, black pepper, red chili, salt and honey. Stir well and garnish with a sprinkle of cumin powder. Serve with vegetables.

Yield: approximately 3 cups

A Taste of India
YOGURT DISHES, SOUPS AND SALADSS

Crunch Spicy Yogurt

2 cups yogurt

1 teaspoon cumin seeds, roasted and ground

1 teaspoon ground black pepper

½ teaspoon salt, or to taste

2-4 green chilies, mild or hot to taste, chopped fine

½ cup milk

1 cup puffed rice

Garnish:

1 tablespoon finely chopped fresh coriander leaves (cilantro)

In a bowl, beat the yogurt with a whisk or an egg beater until it is creamy. Add the black pepper, green chilies, cumin, salt and milk and mix well. Stir in the puffed rice. Garnish with coriander leaves. Chill for half an hour before serving.

Yield: 3 cups

A Taste of India
YOGURT DISHES, SOUPS AND SALADS

Soups and Salads

Yogurt Salad
(PACHAADEE)

A salad with a uniquely Indian taste.

4-5 small potatoes, peeled and diced

1 cup green peas, fresh or frozen

2 tomatoes chopped

½ cup peanuts, ground to a meal

4 green chilies, mild or hot, to taste, chopped

1 sprig fresh coriander leaves (cilantro)

1⅓ cups grated carrots

5 cups yogurt

½ fresh coconut, grated

1½ teaspoons salt, or to taste

2 tablespoons vegetable oil

1/3 cup fresh mung bean sprouts

pinch of black mustard seeds

 Steam the potatoes and peas until tender, about 5 minutes, add peas and steam for one minute longer. In a bowl, mix potatoes with the tomatoes, green chilies, sprouts, carrots, coconut, peanuts, coriander leaves, yogurt and salt.

 In a thick-bottomed frying pan, heat the oil and sauté the black mustard seeds until they start to pop. Add immediately to the yogurt mixture and stir. Serve chilled.

Yield: 9 cups

A Taste of India
YOGURT DISHES, SOUPS AND SALADSS

Curried Cottage Cheese Salad

½ cup onions, sliced into crescents

½ teaspoon salt

2 tablespoons dried (unsweetened) coconut

4 tablespoons hot milk

½ green chili, mild or hot to taste, chopped coarsely

juice of 1 lemon

¼ teaspoon ground black pepper

6 sprigs fresh coriander leaves or watercress, chopped coarsely

½ bell pepper, chopped (optional)

1 cup cottage cheese

① Place the onions in a bowl and sprinkle with salt. Let stand 30 minutes, then pour cold water over them and drain well.

② Soak the coconut in hot milk for 30 minutes, then drain.

③ Mix together all remaining ingredients and stir well. Let stand 30 minutes before serving.

Yield: 2 cups

A Taste of India
YOGURT DISHES, SOUPS AND SALADS

Apple-Vegetable Salad

A most unusual hot salad—colorful and zesty!

1 cup green peas, fresh or frozen

1 small apple

1 medium potato

1 carrot

½ teaspoon mustard powder

½ teaspoon lemon juice

½ teaspoon ground white pepper

3 teaspoons cream

¼ teaspoon salt, or to taste

❶ Steam the peas, carrot, apple and potato separately until each one is tender. Let them cool slightly, then peel the potato, carrot and apple and dice. Transfer to a bowl and add the peas.

❷ In a small bowl, mix together the mustard powder, white pepper, salt, lemon juice and cream. Pour over the vegetables and gently toss. Serve hot.

Yield: about 3½ cups

A Taste of India
YOGURT DISHES, SOUPS AND SALADSS

❦

Cream of Almond Soup

A very delicate soup, good for children recuperating from an illness.

1 cup milk

24 almonds

3 carrots, peeled and cut into small pieces

1-inch piece fresh ginger, sliced

1 pound (about 3 cups) green peas, fresh or frozen

9 cups water

15 black peppercorns

¼–½ teaspoon ground white pepper, to taste

4-5 teaspoons cornstarch

1 teaspoon salt, or to taste

① Boil milk in a small saucepan, then let cool. Transfer cooled milk to a blender add the almonds, and grind together.

② Fill a large pot with the carrots, peas, black peppercorns, fresh ginger and 9 cups of water. Cook over low heat until only 6 cups of water are left, about 10–15 minutes. Use a slotted spoon to remove the vegetables, peppercorns, and ginger from the broth.

③ Add the white pepper to the broth and bring it to a boil. Mix the cornstarch in 1/3 cup of cold water and add it to the boiling broth. Turn down the heat and stir until the mixture starts to thicken slightly. Add the ground almond mixture from the blender; combine.

④ Just before serving, add salt to taste.

Yield: 8 cups

The Holy Man and the Dog

Once there was an old holy man who was noted for his humility. He would sit by the side of the road singing songs of praise to God. Trusting in God to provide for all his needs, he would eat only what was offered to him. When people brought him a morsel or two of food, he would thank them in the name of his Creator and pray for them.

Although he was very well loved and respected, he would sometimes go for several days with barely a piece of bread to eat and a glass of water to drink. People would pass by, seeing him by the roadside singing his simple songs in utter contentment and absorption, and forget that perhaps he was hungry.

On just such a day, at the end of a week of hungry days, the old man was blessed by the generosity of a young woman. It being her birthday, she had cooked much delicious food for distribution to the poor and the needy in thankfulness for the gift of life. When she came to the holy man's spot, she bowed before him and touched his feet. Then she set before him a bag of steaming fresh chapatis and a container of ghee to spread upon them. He smiled and blessed her, and then, with the welcome aroma of fried whole wheat filling his nostrils, began afresh his song of praise.

As the holy man was rising from his spot to begin his walk home, his bag of chapatis in one hand, the ghee in the other, a stray dog of the village came tearing down the road. As it ran by the old man, it tore the bag of chapatis from his hand and made off with them at full speed. The old man, without skipping a beat, took off after him. "Come back, come back," he cried, "those chapatis are dry! Here, have some ghee. It will make them more tasty!"

A traveling merchant who had observed the scene remarked to his companion, "Who was that old man who came running by?" "That was no man," his friend replied, "for no man could care so much more about a stray dog than about his own well-being. That 'old man' we just saw was God Himself."

BREADS

In the villages of northern India, round, thin, unleavened whole-wheat breads are not only the basic food but the primary eating utensil as well. Since almost all vegetarian preparations are either creamy or in small pieces, there is no need for knives. And because of the chapati and thousands of years of practice, forks are obsolete. One simply breaks off a piece of bread, folds it around a bit of food, and scoops it up into one's mouth. And because of traditional hygienic prohibitions, this is all done using only the right hand!

According to yogic philosophy, eating with the hands actually increases the healing nourishment derived from the food. Praana or ambient energy is absorbed directly from the food into the body through the hands. Certainly, this is the method of eating that young children enjoy the most!

For the unpracticed Westerner who does not wish to delve too deeply into Indian culture, Indian breads are simply light, delicious, fresh accompaniments to a meal. When filled with vegetables and fried, they can serve as a light meal by themselves.

In the traditional society of India, those who are preparing the meal may continue turning out light, fluffy, fresh breads, one after another, as many as anyone can eat. Only after everyone is completely satisfied will they sit down to their own meal. This is the ideal way to eat Indian breads, made and served with such selfless devotion and love, hot off the griddle.

If everyone prefers to sit down together, these breads can be made just before the meal, stacked in a bowl lined with a clean cloth, covered, and kept warm in the oven. The cloth absorbs the steam rising off the fresh breads and thus keeps them from becoming soggy.

A Taste of India
BREADS

Successful Indian Bread Making

UTENSILS

- a bowl for mixing dough
- a pastry board or flat surface for kneading and rolling out the dough
- a large, heavy, smooth-surfaced, cast-iron frying pan or griddle for cooking the breads
- a heavy, deep, cast-iron frying pan or wok for deep-frying
- a rolling pin
- a stainless-steel slotted spoon or spatula
- a pair of tongs
- cloth napkins or dish towels
- paper towels

FLOUR

The flour used in most Indian breads is whole-wheat *pastry* flour. Pastry flour is a finer grind of flour than regular whole-wheat flour, with most of the coarse bran flakes ground down. This gives the flour a silky texture especially suited to making soft, smooth unleavened bread.

If you are unable to obtain whole-wheat pastry flour, you can use the whole-wheat flour available in the supermarket, but adjust it by either: (1) sifting it through a fine-meshed sieve to remove the large flakes of bran (you can save these and sprinkle them on cereal), or (2) mixing it with unbleached white all-purpose flour in a ratio of 2 cups of whole-wheat flour to 1 cup of white all-purpose flour *or* using half of each flour, depending on which mixture best makes the bread you like.

Even better than the whole-wheat pastry flour or the blend, however, is a flour made especially for Indian breads. It is available in Indian and some West Indian groceries. It's called *aattaa* and is marketed under the name "Chapati Flour."

A Taste of India
BREADS

SERVING AND STORING

If you want to make a large quantity of chapatis so you don't have to make them fresh each meal, you can cook them on only one side, take them off the griddle, let them cool, and then put them in the refrigerator or the freezer. When you next want to eat them, just dampen the uncooked side with a little water and put it (wet side up) in the oven at 400 degrees or on broil. Very soon the chapati will be soft and a little browned and hot to eat. Just spread with a little butter or ghee.

And if you're traveling and want to take chapatis with you, instead of using water in the dough, use milk. These chapatis stay so soft that they'll keep fresh tasting for a couple of days. Even better for traveling or for lunch boxes are stuffed pranthas. They stay fresh and get even more delicious after a couple of days.

A Taste of India
BREADS

Chapatis
(CHAPAATEE)

2 ½ cups of whole-wheat pastry flour or chapati flour

1 cup water (or more as needed for consistency of dough)

2 tablespoons ghee or olive oil

To make the dough:

① Place 2 cups of flour in a bowl. Make a well in the center. Pour the water into the well, gradually mixing the flour into the water to form a soft dough. Mix until a compact mass is formed. If the dough is too crumbly, add a little more water.

② Transfer the dough to a flat surface and knead it for 5 minutes, until the dough is soft and smooth and pliable. Add more flour if needed to keep dough from sticking to surface. Then put the dough back into a bowl, cover with a damp cloth and let it rest for 15 to 20 minutes.

To make chapatis:

① Knead the dough a few more times. Break off a piece of dough (about one-sixth of the whole) and roll it between your palms to form a small ball about 1½ inches in diameter (see figure 1).

② Place the dough ball on a lightly floured pastry board or flat surface. Using a rolling pin, roll into a circle about 6 to 9 inches in diameter, 1/8 inch thick (see figure 2).

To cook the chapatis:

① Carefully lift the chapati and place it onto a hot griddle or cast-iron frying pan. Cook until the top surface starts to form little bubbles, about 20 to 30 seconds. Immediately flip it over with

A Taste of India
BREADS

a pair of tongs or a spatula and cook the other side until it browns, 8 to 10 seconds. (If you are cooking on a gas stove, you may get best results by first placing the chapati directly on a burner over a medium flame.)

2 Using a clean cloth or napkin, press it gently in the center. The chapati should puff up like a balloon When it puffs up like that it is known as a *phulka*.

3 Place the cooked chapati on a clean cloth and spread lightly with ghee or butter. Serve hot.

Clean any flour off the griddle or pan after cooking each chapati.

Yield: 6 chapatis

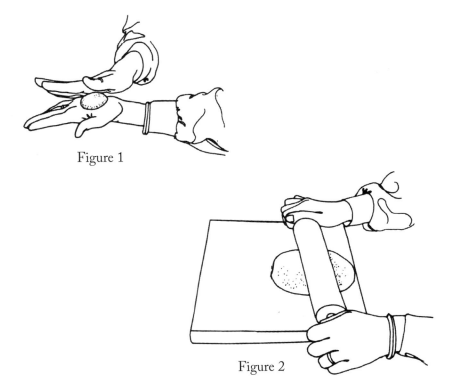

Figure 1

Figure 2

A Taste of India
BREADS

Plain Pranthas
(PARAANTHAA)

1 cup whole-wheat pastry flour or chapati flour

¼ cup ghee or butter for spreading

½ teaspoon salt (optional)

½ cup water

To make the dough:

1. Place the flour and salt in a bowl. Make a well in the center. Pour the water into the well gradually, mixing the flour into the water to form a soft dough. Mix until a compact mass of dough is formed.

2. Transfer the dough to a flat surface and knead for 5 minutes, until the dough is soft and smooth and pliable. Then put the dough back into a bowl, cover with a damp cloth, and let it rest for 15 to 20 minutes.

To make the pranthas:

1. Knead the rested dough a few more times. Break off a piece of dough (about ¼ of the whole) and roll it between your hands to make a small ball about 1½ inches in diameter.

2. Place the dough ball on a lightly floured pastry board or other flat surface. Using a rolling pin, roll into a circle about inches in diameter, 1/8 inch thick.

3. Lightly spread ghee or butter on the raw circle, fold it in half, and then spread the upper surface with more butter or ghee. Fold it again, either in half or in thirds, and roll it into a ball again. Lightly flour dough ball, if necessary, and roll the dough out again into a circle about 5 inches in diameter, 1/8 inch thick.

A Taste of India
BREADS

To cook the pranthas:

1. Carefully place a prantha onto a hot griddle or cast-iron frying pan. Cook until the top surface starts to form little bubbles, about 20 to 30 seconds. Immediately flip it over to brown on the other side, for about 8 to 10 seconds.

2. When both sides are cooked, spread 1 teaspoon of ghee or butter on each side, and fry each side once more until golden brown. Serve hot.

Clean excess flour off griddle after cooking each prantha.

Yield: 4 pranthas

A Taste of India
BREADS

❧

Stuffed Pranthas

I include two methods for rolling the stuffed pranthas; use whichever seems most natural to you.

For the dough:

1 cup whole-wheat pastry flour

½ teaspoon salt (optional)

½ cup water

For the filling:

2 teaspoons chopped green chilies, mild or hot, to taste

2 tablespoons finely chopped peeled fresh ginger

1 medium onion, grated

1 teaspoon oregano (ajwan) or celery seeds

1 teaspoon garlic powder

1 teaspoon red chili powder or ground black pepper

To make the dough:

Follow the directions in the recipe for plain pranthas.

To make the filling:

In a large bowl, mix together all filling ingredients. Use your hands to squeeze out all the liquid; the mixture should be very dry.

To make the stuffed pranthas:

METHOD 1

1 Knead the dough a few more times, then separate it into 3 portions. Roll a portion between your palms to make a small ball about 1½ inches in diameter (see figure 1).

2 Place the dough ball on a lightly floured pastry board or other flat surface. Using a rolling pin, roll into a small thick circle about 3 to 6 inches in diameter.

3 Place a portion of the filling in the center of the circle (see figure 3). Fold over the edges of the dough to cover the filling (see figure 4). If the dough breaks while folding, repair it by placing a little piece of dough over the hole.

4 Carefully roll the dough into a circle about 5 inches in diameter, 1/8 inch thick.

A Taste of India
BREADS

about 3¼ cups finely grated white radishes, cauliflower, carrots, or boiled and mashed potatoes (equivalent to 2 medium potatoes, 4 medium carrots, or ½ large cauliflower)

½ teaspoon salt, or to taste

½ cup ghee or butter for spreading

METHOD 2

1. Roll dough into 6 small circles, each about 3 or 4 inches in diameter.

2. Place a portion of the filling on one circle. Cover it with another circle.

3. Flatten this "sandwich" with your hands. Then roll out carefully with a rolling pin. The finished prantha should be about 5 inches in diameter and 1/8 inch thick. Repeat with remaining circles, making 3 stuffed prantha in all.

To cook the stuffed pranthas:

1. Carefully place a stuffed prantha onto a hot griddle or cast-iron frying pan. Cook for 1 minute on each side.

2. Spread 1 tablespoon of ghee or butter on each side of the prantha and fry each side until crisp and golden brown.

3. When both sides are cooked, spread again with ghee or butter.

Serve hot with yogurt.

Yield: 3 stuffed pranthas

Figure 3

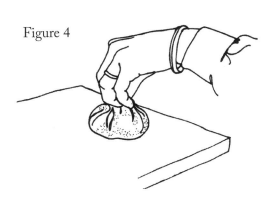

Figure 4

A Taste of India
BREADS

Puffed Bread
(PATHURAA)

Serve these thick, bland pancakes with chickpeas or Camritsari Chole.

2 medium potatoes, grated

1 teaspoon salt, or to taste

2½ cups unbleached white flour (approximately; enough to hold the potatoes together into a dough)

2 cups vegetable oil or ghee for deep-frying

To make the dough:

Place the grated potatoes in a bowl. Add enough flour and salt to form a dough. Mix well. Let the dough rest in a warm place for 30 minutes.

To make the pathuras:

1. Break off a piece of dough and roll it between your palms to form a small ball about 1½ inches in diameter.

2. Place the dough ball on a lightly floured pastry board or other flat surface. Using a rolling pin, roll into a circle about 6 to 8 inches in diameter. Repeat using remaining dough; you should have enough for about 15 pathuras.

3. In a deep thick-bottomed frying pan or wok, heat the oil or ghee to smoking point.

4. Carefully immerse the pathura one at a time into the hot oil or ghee and fry until golden brown.

5. Remove from the oil with a slotted spoon, letting the excess oil drip back into the pan.

Serve hot with chutney.

Yield: 15 pathuras

A Taste of India
BREADS

Puris
(POOREE)

2 cups whole-wheat pastry flour or chapati flour

½ cup water

2 cups ghee or vegetable oil (for deep-frying)

To make the dough:

1. Follow directions for making chapatis.

2. Knead the dough a few more times. Break off a piece of dough and roll it between your palms to form a small ball about 1 inch in diameter.

3. Place the dough ball onto a lightly floured pastry board or other flat surface. Using a rolling pin, roll out into a circle about 3 inches in diameter, 1/8 inch thick. Repeat with remaining dough.

To cook the puris:

1. In a deep thick-bottomed pan or wok, heat the vegetable oil or ghee to smoking point.

2. Immerse a puri in the oil or ghee and press down lightly in the center with a flat spoon. When the puri floats back up to the surface and puffs up like a balloon, carefully turn it over with a spoon. Fry until it is golden brown. Then remove the puri with a slotted spoon, letting the excess oil drip back into the pan. Place the cooked puri on a plate lined with paper towels to remove any extra oil. Fry the remaining puris in this fashion.

Serve very hot with any curry or with honey.

Yield: 10–12 puris

A Taste of India
BREADS

Stuffed Puris
(MASAALEWAALEE POOREE)

You will need to begin making the yeast for this dough at least one full day in advance, so plan accordingly.

For the yeast for the dough:

½ cup unbleached white flour

¼ teaspoon baking soda

2 teaspoons yogurt

½–¾ cups lukewarm water

Other prep:

1 cup split black mung beans, washed well 4 cups water

For the dough:

2½ cups unbleached white flour, plus additional for dusting

½–¾ cups lukewarm water

To make the yeast for the dough:

 Mix the unbleached white flour, yogurt, baking soda and lukewarm water together in a bowl and *keep it in a warm place, covered, for at least 24 hours* (in winter, keep it for 2 days).

Other preparations:

Soak the split black mung beans in the water *overnight*.

To make the dough:

 Place 2½ cups flour in a bowl and make a well in the center. Gradually add the prepared yeast and ½ cup lukewarm water into the well, adding a bit more water if needed to form a soft dough. Mix until a compact ball of dough is formed.

 Place the dough on a lightly floured flat surface and knead for 5 minutes, adding flour to keep dough from sticking. Put the dough in a clean bowl, sprinkle the top with a little water and oil, and cover with a damp cloth. Let the dough rise until it doubles in size, about 1½ hours.

To make the filling:

 Drain the water off the mung beans. Transfer the beans to a blender and process until a thick paste is formed. Add the chili powder, garam masala, salt and 4 cups of water and mix well.

A Taste of India
BREADS

For the filling:

2 teaspoons red chili powder

4 cups water

2 teaspoons garam masala

¼ cup vegetable oil or ghee

½ teaspoon salt, or to taste

2 cups vegetable oil or ghee for deep-frying

2 In a thick-bottomed frying pan, heat ¼ cup oil or ghee and sauté this paste until the beans stick together in one mass and separate from the sides of the pan, about 20 minutes. Set aside to cool.

To make the stuffed puris:

1 Punch down the dough, kneading it again with a little water added to keep it pliable.

2 Break off a piece of dough and, with wet hands, form it into a small ball about 1½ inches in diameter.

3 Place the dough ball onto a lightly floured pastry board or flat surface. Using a rolling pin, roll out halfway. Place about 2 tablespoons of the bean filling in the center and fold the edges of the dough up over the filling.

4 Using your hands, carefully press the filled ball into small pancakes about 3 inches in diameter.

To cook the stuffed puris:

1 In a deep thick-bottomed frying pan or wok, heat the 2 cups of vegetable oil or ghee.

2 Carefully immerse a raw stuffed puri into the oil or ghee and press down very lightly in the center with a flat spoon. When the puri floats back up to the surface and puffs up like a balloon, carefully turn it over with the spoon. Fry it until it is golden brown. Then remove the puri with a slotted spoon, letting the excess oil drip back into the pan. Place the cooked puri on a plate lined with paper towels to remove any extra oil. Serve very hot.

Yield: 20 stuffed puris

RICE DISHES

In south and east India, rice (chaawal) is almost as essential to eating as chewing; every mouthful of food is usually accompanied by a bite of rice. The rice serves as a filling and coarsely textured contrast to the spicier and saucier vegetable or bean dishes. In the north, where wheat is more plentiful, bread serves much the same purpose.

India produces more than one thousand varieties of rice. The rice I recommend for my recipes is basmati rice, a long-grained, white, slightly nutty-tasting rice. It is available in all Indian food stores and some natural food stores. Texmati rice, which is grown in the United States and tastes similar to basmati, may also be used. However, Texmati rice tends to break up into smaller grains while cooking, which will give a different texture to the dishes.

Rice complements most dishes that are soupy or made with gravy.

A Taste of India
RICE DISHES

Plain Fried Rice
(CHAAWAL)

2 cups rice

4 tablespoons vegetable oil or ghee

6 cloves garlic, chopped

2 tablespoons finely chopped peeled fresh ginger

2 medium onions, chopped

4 whole cloves

¾ teaspoon salt, or to taste

1 small cinnamon stick

4 cups water

6 black peppercorns

4 green cardamom pods (use only the seeds)

1 Carefully wash and drain the rice.

2 In a large thick-bottomed pot, heat the vegetable oil or ghee and fry the onion, garlic and ginger until golden brown. Add the cloves, cinnamon, black peppercorns, cardamom and salt and fry for 1 more minute. Add the rice, stir and fry for 2 minutes more. Next, add the water, cover and bring to a boil. Immediately turn down the heat and simmer until the rice is tender and the water is absorbed.

3 Turn off the heat, keep covered and let sit for 5 minutes.

Serve with a curry, yogurt or raita.

Yield: 4½ cups

A Taste of India
RICE DISHES

Vegetable Rice
(BIRYAANEE)

½ cup vegetable oil or ghee

½ cup panir, cubed

1 large onion, chopped

2 teaspoons crushed red chilies

3 whole cloves

2 teaspoons ground cumin powder

1 small cinnamon stick

4 green cardamom pods (use only the seeds)

2½ teaspoons salt

1 cup green peas, fresh or frozen

2 tablespoons almonds, soaked and peeled

1 large carrot, chopped

4 cups water

2 cups rice

1 bay leaf

1 cup milk

Optional garnish:

¼ teaspoon kewra essence*

2 silver leaves*

① In a large thick-bottomed pot, heat the vegetable oil or ghee and fry the panir cubes until they are light brown. Then remove them and set aside.

② In this oil, fry the onions until light brown. Add the cloves, cumin, cardamom seeds, red chilies, cinnamon and salt and stir well, continuing to fry until the onions are brown. Add the peas, carrots, almonds and fried panir and fry for a few more minutes. Add the water and bring to a boil.

③ Wash the rice thoroughly and drain. Add the rice, milk and bay leaf to the boiling mixture and let it come to a boil again. Then cover, reduce to low heat, and cook until the rice is tender and all the liquid is absorbed, about 15 to 20 minutes.

④ Keep covered, remove from the heat, and let sit for 10 minutes. Before serving, remove cinnamon stick and, if desired, sprinkle with kewra essence and decorate with silver leaf.

Yield: 10 cups

*See "Special Ingredients and Where to Find Them," page 258.

A Taste of India
RICE DISHES

Mixed Vegetable Rice
(PILAAO)

This mild side dish goes well with a spicy vegetable or bean dish. I offer two variations.

Recipe 1

2 cups rice

4 cups water

4 tablespoons vegetable oil or ghee

1 small cinnamon stick

8 whole black peppercorns

1 teaspoon cumin seeds

1 teaspoon salt, or to taste

6 whole cloves

1 cup green peas, fresh or frozen

1 cup green beans, chopped

1 cup cauliflower, cut into small pieces

1 cup carrots, peeled and sliced thin

Recipe 1

① Carefully wash and drain the rice. In a large thick-bottomed pot, bring 4 cups of water to a boil, add the rice and let it come to a boil again. Lower the heat and simmer until the rice is tender and all the water is absorbed. Remove from the heat.

② In a large thick-bottomed frying pan, heat the vegetable oil or ghee and add the cumin, cloves, cinnamon, black peppercorns and salt and stir well. Lower the heat and add the peas, carrots, green beans and cauliflower. Cover and simmer for 5 minutes.

③ Add the vegetable/spice mixture to the cooked rice, stir well, and warm over low heat for 3 minutes. Fluff with a fork and remove the cinnamon stick before serving.

A Taste of India
RICE DISHES

Recipe 2

As in Recipe 1, plus:

2 medium onions, chopped

2 tablespoons peeled and finely chopped fresh ginger

6 cloves garlic, chopped

Recipe 2

 Carefully wash and drain the rice

 In a large, thick-bottomed frying pan or wok, heat the vegetable oil or ghee and fry the onions, garlic and ginger until golden brown. Add the green peas, carrots, green beans and cauliflower and stir well. Turn heat to low, cover the pan, and cook for 5 minutes.

3. Add the cumin, cloves, cinnamon, black peppercorns and salt and fry for 1 minute. Add the rice and fry, stirring continuously, for 1 minute. Next, add the water, bring to a boil, cover, and cook over low heat until the rice is tender and all the water absorbed, about 15–20 minutes. Turn off the heat, but keep the pan covered for 5 more minutes. Remove the cinnamon stick and serve with plain yogurt.

Yield: about 8 cups

A Taste of India
RICE DISHES

❦

Sweet Yellow Rice
(ZARDAA PILAAO)

A fancy dish for formal occasions. Very sweet.

1 cup rice

⅓ cup water

a pinch of saffron (for color)

⅓ cup honey

2 tablespoons vegetable oil or ghee

2½ cups water

green cardamom pods (use the seeds only)

½ cup milk

¼ teaspoon kewra essence (optional)

Decoration:

silver leaf (optional)

¼ cup khoa (optional)

1 tablespoon chopped pistachio nuts, unsalted or salt washed off

milk or unsweetened evaporated milk

2 tablespoons date sugar

1 tablespoon raisins, soaked in hot water for 10 minutes

① Carefully wash and drain the rice.

② In a saucepan, bring 1/3 cup of water and honey to a boil. Add a pinch of saffron. Keep boiling and stirring until it is a sticky syrup. Put aside to cool.

③ In a large thick-bottomed pot, heat the vegetable oil or ghee and briefly fry the green cardamom seeds and rice. Immediately add 2½ cups of water. Cover, bring to a boil, then lower to simmer and cook until all the water is absorbed, about 20 minutes.

④ Mix the honey syrup (step 2) and milk into the cooked rice. Replace the cover and continue cooking until the milk and syrup are absorbed and the rice is tender. Add the (optional) kewra essence and stir.

⑤ Place in a serving dish and, if desired, decorate with silver leaf. Mix the khoa or evaporated milk with the date sugar and sprinkle over rice, then top with pistachios and raisins.

Yield: approximately 3 cups

A Taste of India
RICE DISHES

Rice and Mung Beans
(KICHAREE)

A solid staple of the traditional Indian diet—fortifying and mildly spicy. Good with plain yogurt.

1 cup whole green mung beans

16 cups water

2-3 teaspoons salt, to taste

2 cups rice

½ cup vegetable oil or ghee

4-inch piece of fresh ginger, peeled and chopped fine

2 medium onions, chopped

8 cloves garlic, chopped

1 small cinnamon stick

1 teaspoon cumin seeds

6 whole cloves

½ teaspoon ground black pepper, or to taste

4 green cardamom pods

① Carefully pick over the beans and wash them. Wash the rice and drain. Mix the rice and beans together with the water and salt in a large thick-bottomed pot. Cook until the beans are soft and split open and the mixture has the consistency of a thick soup.

② In a thick-bottomed frying pan, heat the oil or ghee and fry the onion, garlic and ginger until light brown. Add the cinnamon, cloves, green cardamom, cumin and black pepper and fry for 1 minute. Add this mixture to the cooked rice and beans, stir, and cook for 2–3 minutes over low heat. Serve with plain yogurt.

Yield: 14 cups

A Taste of India
RICE DISHES

Split Chickpea and Fruit Rice
(CHANAA DAAL PHAL BIRYAANEE)

Split chickpeas:

½ cup split chickpeas (garbanzo beans)

¼ teaspoon salt, or to taste

2 cups water

2 bay leaves

2 tablespoons vegetable oil or ghee

2 tablespoons cashew nuts

6 firm (not mushy) dates, cut in long, thin slices

2 teaspoons garam masala

Rice:

½ cup rice

1½ cups water

3 tablespoons vegetable oil or ghee

¼ teaspoon ground cinnamon

1 medium onion, cut in rounds

To prepare the split chickpeas:

1 Thoroughly pick over and wash the beans. Soak in 2 cups of water for 1 hour. Add ¼ teaspoon salt and the bay leaves to the water and boil until the beans are soft, about 30 minutes. Drain off the water.

2 In a large thick-bottomed frying pan or wok, heat 2 tablespoons of vegetable oil or ghee and add the garam masala, cashew nuts and dates. Mix in the cooked chickpeas and simmer until hot.

To prepare the rice:

1 Thoroughly wash the rice and drain. In a bowl, soak the rice in 1½ cups of water for 15 minutes. Then drain, but save the water for cooking.

2 In a large thick-bottomed frying pan or wok, heat 3 tablespoons of vegetable oil or ghee and sauté the onion until brown. Add the red chili, green cardamom, cinnamon, cumin, salt and the reserved water from the rice. Bring to a boil. Add the rice and milk and cook until all the liquid evaporates and the rice is tender. Remove from the heat.

A Taste of India
RICE DISHES

1½ teaspoons ground cumin

¼ teaspoon salt, or to taste

½ teaspoon crushed dry red chilies

½ cup milk

4 green cardamom pods (use only the seeds)

Garnish:

2 thin slices whole-wheat bread

3–4 cashews, chopped

1 medium tomato, sliced thin

1 tablespoon vegetable oil or ghee

To serve:

1. Cut the bread into cubes and fry in 1 tablespoon of vegetable oil or ghee until brown.

2. Place the rice in a serving dish. Pour the chickpea mixture over it. Top with the bread cubes, chopped cashews and the sliced tomatoes.

Yield: about 3 cups

A Taste of India
RICE DISHES

Coconut Rice

2 cups rice

2 cups grated fresh coconut

4 cups water

2 tablespoons vegetable oil or ghee

4 whole cloves

4 green cardamom pods (use only the seeds)

4 medium onions, chopped

1 small cinnamon stick

1 teaspoon salt, or to taste

1. Wash the rice thoroughly, drain and set aside.

2. In an electric blender, blend the coconut with the water until smooth. Set aside.

3. In a large thick-bottomed saucepan, heat the vegetable oil or ghee and fry the onions until golden brown. Add the cinnamon, cloves, green cardamom and salt. Fry for 1 minute, then add the coconut-water mixture and rice. Cover and bring to a boil, lower the heat and simmer until the rice is tender and the liquid absorbed, about 15–20 minutes. Turn off the heat but keep the rice covered for another 5 minutes before serving.

Yield: 5 cups rice

A Taste of India
RICE DISHES

Creamy Cheese and Pea Vegetable Rice
(PANEER MATAR PILAAO)

Children as well as adults love this dish!

2 cups rice

2 tablespoons vegetable oil or ghee

½ cup panir, cubed

1 onion, sliced in thin crescents

4 green cardamom pods (use only the seeds)

2 bay leaves

½ teaspoon red chili powder

3 whole cloves

2 teaspoons ground white cumin

1 cup green peas, fresh or frozen

¼ teaspoon ground cinnamon

3 cups water

1 teaspoon salt

① Carefully wash and drain the rice.

② In a large thick-bottomed frying pan, heat oil or ghee and fry the panir cubes until light brown. Remove from the oil and set aside.

③ In the same oil, fry the onions, bay leaves and green cardamom seeds until the onions are golden brown. Add the red chili, white cumin, cinnamon and cloves, peas, fried panir and water. Bring these ingredients to a boil.

④ Add the rice and salt, cover and cook over low heat until the water is absorbed and each grain of rice is separate, about 20 minutes. Keep covered, remove from the heat, and let stand for 15 minutes before serving.

Yield: 7 cups

A Taste of India
RICE DISHES

Royal Sweet Rice
(SHAAHEE MITHEE PILAAO)

2 cups rice

½ cup vegetable oil or ghee

1½ cups water

6 green cardamom pods (use only the seeds)

¾ cup honey

½ teaspoon kewra essence (optional)

2 tablespoons almonds, soaked and peeled

silver leaf (for decoration; optional)

2 tablespoons pistachios, unsalted or salt washed off

½ cup khoa or unsweetened evaporated milk

1 Wash the rice carefully, drain, and then cover with water and soak for 15 minutes. Rinse again and drain.

2 In a large thick-bottomed saucepan, heat the oil or ghee and briefly fry the cardamom seeds and rice. Add 1½ cups of water, bring to a boil, then cover and cook over low heat until the rice is tender and all the water is absorbed, about 15 minutes.

3 Stir in the honey and (optional) kewra essence and cook over very low heat until absorbed, about 20 minutes. Stir in the almonds, pistachios and khoa or evaporated milk. If desired, decorate with silver leaf. Cover and let sit for 5-10 minutes before serving.

Yield: about 6 cups

The Emperor Comes to Dinner

The Mughal Emperor Akbar was well known as a patron of artists, musicians and holy men. When he heard of the spiritual greatness of Guru Amar Das, he decided at once to pay him a visit. Guru Amar Das had decreed that anyone wishing to see him must first sit and eat at the Guru's langar, where rich and poor sat side by side and were served equally.

When word reached the Guru's court that the Emperor was on his way, there was great speculation as to whether he too would be expected to obey the Guru's order. After all, to offend a king carried no small penalty in those days. Nonetheless, Guru Amar Das was unwavering. Even Akbar the Great would partake of the Guru's kitchen!

When Akbar finally arrived, he proved that his wisdom was worthy of his reputation. He instructed his courtiers and retainers to join him as he sat in line upon the stone floor and was served a simple meal of vegetables and yogurt, dahl cooked in ghee, and steaming hot chapatis. He shared his dinner that night with Sikhs, Muslims and Hindus of all castes and classes.

So pleased was the Emperor by the tastiness of the simple feast—flavored with love and selfless service—and by the living example of sharing and equality, that he offered the Guru a large tract of land as a token of his esteem.

"But, Sir," the Guru replied, "to accept such a gift from a king would not be right. People might think that I am beholden to you, whereas I pledge my allegiance to the One God alone."

"In that case," Akbar replied, "the land shall be granted to your lovely daughter, for she is the image of gracefulness and service. Now that is an offer you cannot refuse!"

Years later, the land which was granted by Akbar became a shrine and site of spiritual healing. A pond was excavated and, in its center, a temple of marble and gold was erected. Today, at the Golden Temple in the city of Amritsar, up to 100,000 people are fed each day in the Guru's langar.

BEAN DISHES

Bean dishes (dahl) provide India with much of its protein. Like rice, the varieties of beans, lentils and dried peas are nearly endless, and their uses endlessly creative—from soups to flours to main dishes to sweets. For most of the recipes given in this chapter, you can experiment and try substituting different kinds of beans and see what you come up with.

In cooking beans, the important thing is to make sure the beans are very well cleaned and very well cooked. Pick out all the little stones and pebbles and wash thoroughly. Thorough cooking helps reduce intestinal gas, as does fresh ginger, which is included in most dahl recipes. In addition, chewing on a green cardamom pod after a meal or having a cup of mint tea helps avoid gas.

There is a shortcut to the overnight soaking that many beans require. Just boil the beans in salted water for 10 minutes. Then immerse them in cold water for one hour. From that point most beans are ready to start the regular cooking procedure called for in the recipe.

Another shortcut is to cook the beans in a pressure cooker. The cooking time will be shorter and the beans themselves creamier and even more delicious.

Bean dishes complement dry (not soupy) vegetable dishes. Bean dishes such as chickpeas and kidney beans are easy to prepare and good to serve for large gatherings.

When serving beans, you may wish to include one bowl of finely chopped jalapeno peppers and/or one bowl of finely chopped onions as a do-it-yourself garnish on your table. That way each person can add zest to his or her beans as taste dictates.

A Taste of India
BEAN DISHES

Cholay

(CHOLE)

Chickpeas (also known as garbanzo beans) and potatoes are a winning combination. This very filling, flavorful dish is a north Indian standard.

For the beans:

2 cups chickpeas (garbanzo beans)

1½ teaspoons baking soda

2 teaspoons salt

3 whole cloves

10 cups water

2 green cardamom pods (use only the seeds)

For the sauce:

2 medium potatoes, boiled, peeled and cut into medium-sized pieces

4 teaspoons ground black pepper

4 teaspoons mango powder

½ cup peeled and sliced fresh ginger (long thin slices are best)

To prepare the chickpeas:

1. Carefully pick over and wash the beans and drain. In a large pot, *soak them overnight* in 10 cups of water, along with the cloves, green cardamom seeds and baking soda.

2. Cook chickpeas over low heat in the same water, with salt added, until they are tender, about 30–45 minutes. Drain off and discard the liquid and set the chickpeas aside.

To make the sauce:

1. In a large thick-bottomed frying pan or wok, mix together the cooked chickpeas and all the sauce ingredients. Cook over low heat, stirring well so that the spices are thoroughly mixed in.

2. Remove from the heat. Place in a serving bowl.

A Taste of India
BEAN DISHES

4 teaspoons ground cumin

4 teaspoons garam masala

1 onion, sliced

1 teaspoon salt, or to taste

Garnish:

6 teaspoons chopped fresh coriander leaves (cilantro), chopped

½ cup hot ghee

2 tomatoes, sliced

2 green chilies, mild or hot

4 lemons, washed and sliced thin

 Sprinkle coriander leaves and green chilies on top. Then make a hollow in the center and pour in the hot ghee. Decorate with tomato and lemon slices.

Yield: 7–8 cups

A Taste of India
BEAN DISHES

Mung Bean Dahl
(MOONG KEE DAAL)

½ pound green mung beans (whole)

6 cups water

½ teaspoon salt, or to taste

1 medium onion, chopped

1 teaspoon ground turmeric

1-inch piece fresh ginger, peeled and finely chopped

1 teaspoon red chili powder

4 tablespoons vegetable oil or ghee

1 teaspoon garam masala

Optional garnish:

½ cup finely chopped jalapeno peppers

½ cup finely chopped onions

① Carefully pick over and wash the beans. Bring the water to a boil and add the beans and salt. Cover and cook over medium heat. When the beans start to split open, add the turmeric and red chili and cook until it has a thick, soupy consistency. Stir frequently to prevent sticking. *Or* pressure cook for ½ hour with 5 cups water, adding turmeric and red chili (after releasing the pressure) halfway through.

② In a thick-bottomed frying pan, heat the vegetable oil or ghee and sauté the onion and ginger until golden brown. Stir in the garam masala and add this mixture to the cooked beans.

③ If you like, garnish with chopped jalapenos and onions.

Yield: 5 cups

A Taste of India
BEAN DISHES

Black Bean Dahl
(MAKEE DAAL DULEE)

1 cup whole black beans

1½–2 teaspoons salt

6 cups water

1 teaspoon ground turmeric

½ cup vegetable oil or ghee

1 tablespoon peeled and finely chopped fresh ginger

1 medium onion, chopped

1½ teaspoons ground cumin

1 teaspoon ground black pepper

2 green chilies, mild or hot, to taste, chopped

1 medium tomato, chopped

2 teaspoons chopped fresh coriander leaves (cilantro)

① Carefully pick over and wash the beans. Soak in 6 cups of water for 10 minutes. Then add the salt and turmeric and boil until the beans are soft yet each bean still remains separate, about 30 minutes. Remove from the heat. *Or beans can be pressure cooked in 5 cups water for ½ hour.*

② In a large thick-bottomed frying pan or wok, heat the vegetable oil and ghee. Sauté the onions and ginger until light brown. Add the cooked beans, cumin, chilies, coriander leaves, black pepper and tomato. Stir and cook for 2 more minutes.

Yield: 5 cups

A Taste of India
BEAN DISHES

Black Beans with Cream
(MAKHNEE URAD DAAL)

Serve this mild but still somewhat spicy (hot) dish with a flavorful dish such as Pumpkin Bartha.

1 pound (about 2½ cups) split black mung beans (urad dahl)

1 teaspoon chopped garlic

6 green chilies, mild or hot, to taste, chopped fine

1 tablespoon peeled and chopped fresh ginger

½ teaspoon baking soda

2-3 teaspoons salt, or to taste

2½ quarts of water

½ cup vegetable oil or ghee

4 medium onions, chopped

4 medium tomatoes, chopped

1 teaspoon crushed dry red chilies

½ cup yogurt

½ cup cream

① Carefully pick over and wash the beans. In a large thick-bottomed pot, cook the beans, ginger, garlic, green chilies, baking soda and salt in 2½ quarts of water over low heat until the beans are soft, about 1 hour.

② In a thick-bottomed frying pan, heat the ghee or vegetable oil and fry the onions until light brown. Add the tomatoes, yogurt, cream and crushed red chilies and cook until the oil starts to separate out. Cook 5 minutes more, stirring frequently.

③ Add the spice mixture to the cooked beans and cook for 5 minutes more. If mixture is too thick, add 1 cup of hot water and cook a few more minutes, until desired consistency is reached.

A Taste of India
BEAN DISHES

Garnish:

1 tablespoon chopped fresh

2 tablespoons chopped almonds coriander leaves (cilantro)

2 tablespoons raisins

Garnish with coriander leaves, raisins and chopped almonds.

Yield: 12–14 cups

A Taste of India
BEAN DISHES

Saucy Chickpeas
(KHATAA CHANAA)

For the beans:

2⅓ cups chickpeas (garbanzo beans)

1 teaspoon baking soda

1 black tea bag

5 cups water

2 teaspoons salt

For the sauce:

2 medium potatoes, boiled, peeled and diced

4 teaspoons turmeric

8 black peppercorns

½ cup peeled and thinly sliced fresh ginger

4 teaspoons ground cumin

3 tablespoons garam masala

8 green chilies, mild or hot, to taste, chopped

2 teaspoons salt

2 tablespoons pomegranate seeds

1 cup hot ghee

To prepare the beans:

① Carefully pick over and wash the beans. *Soak them overnight* in 5 cups of water, along with the baking soda and black tea bag.

② In the same water, cook the beans, along with ½ teaspoon salt, over low heat until tender. Strain off the liquid, reserving it for the sauce.

To make the sauce:

In a large thick-bottomed frying pan or wok, mix together the cooked beans, potatoes, ginger (sauté ginger first, if you prefer), green chilies, pomegranate seeds, turmeric, peppercorns, cumin, garam masala and salt. Make a hollow in the center and into it pour approximately 2 cups of the water from the cooked beans. Bring it to a boil and mix in the spices and the beans. Pour very hot ghee on top of it and let it simmer for 2 minutes.

A Taste of India
BEAN DISHES

Garnish:

a few fresh coriander leaves (cilantro)

2 onions, sliced thin

1 cup chopped tomatoes

4 lemons, sliced

To serve:

Place in a serving dish and garnish with coriander leaves, tomatoes, onions and lemon slices.

Yield: 11 cups

A Taste of India
BEAN DISHES

Kidney Bean Dahl
(RAAJ MAAH)

Very good with plain rice and raita.

Ingredients:

½ pound (about 1⅓ cups) red kidney beans

6 cups water

4 onions

6 cloves garlic, sliced

1-inch piece of fresh ginger, peeled and chopped

4 tablespoons vegetable oil or ghee

1½ teaspoons salt, or to taste

1 tomato, sliced

1 tablespoon water

1 teaspoon crushed dry red chilies

Garnish:

1 teaspoon garam masala

a few fresh coriander leaves (cilantro), chopped

Instructions:

1. Carefully pick over and wash the beans. *Soak overnight* in water. Drain.

2. In an electric blender, blend together the onions, ginger and garlic until they form a paste.

3. In a large thick-bottomed frying pan or wok, heat the vegetable oil or ghee and fry the paste until it is golden brown, stirring continuously to prevent sticking. Stir in 1 tablespoon of water and add the dry red chilies, salt and tomato. Cook until the oil starts to separate out.

4. Add the beans and mix well. Add 6 cups of water and cook over medium heat until the beans are mushy (otherwise they will be indigestible.) *Or* pressure cook for 25–30 minutes using 5½ cups water.

5. To serve, sprinkle with garam masala and coriander leaves.

Yield: 5–6 cups

RELISHES AND PICKLES

Relishes (chutneys) and pickles (achaar) are the exclamation points of Indian food. They are perky little extras that bring a sparkle to the palate. At nearly every Indian meal or snack, there are one or two chutneys to add taste and variety.

Some relishes can be prepared in advance and stored, while others should be served soon after they are made. Chutneys made with herbs, like Mint Chutney, keep for a few days in the refrigerator. Vegetable chutneys, like Carrot Chutney, should be prepared just before serving. Pickles and fruit chutneys can be kept in jars in the refrigerator for a long time.

A Taste of India
RELISHES AND PICKLES

Carrot Chutney
(GAAJAR KEE CHATNEE)

A tangy sweet-and-sour side dish.

1 cup grated carrots

2 tablespoons peeled and chopped fresh ginger

1 cup water

2 cloves garlic, chopped fine

1 cup cider vinegar

2 teaspoons salt

¾ cup honey

1 tablespoon cornstarch

½ teaspoon green cardamom seeds

¼ cup cashew nuts or 8 soaked, peeled almonds

½ teaspoon red chili powder

2 teaspoons raisins (soak in water for 10 minutes, then drain)

① Place the carrots, water, garlic and ginger in a saucepan and cook until the carrots are tender and all the water has evaporated, about 10 minutes.

② Add the vinegar, honey, cardamom seeds, red chili, salt, cornstarch and nuts and cook until the mixture is golden brown and slightly thick about 15 minutes. Add the raisins and cook for a few minutes to combine the flavors.

③ Let cool and store in a covered jar in the refrigerator.

Yield: about 2½ cups

A Taste of India

RELISHES AND PICKLES

Yogurt Chutney
(DAHEE CHATNEE)

Spicy and fresh tasting—very refreshing!

½ cup fresh mint leaves

3 teaspoons mango powder

3 green chilies, mild or hot, to taste

¼ teaspoon salt, or to taste

½ cup yogurt

1. In an electric blender, blend together the mint leaves, green chilies, mango powder and salt (add a little water if necessary to get it to blend).

2. In a bowl, beat the yogurt with a whisk or an egg beater so it is creamy. Add the blended ingredients and stir well.

Yield: ¾–1 cup

A Taste of India
RELISHES AND PICKLES

Tomato Chutney
(TAMAATAR CHATNEE)

The Indian version of America's favorite chutney—ketchup!

1 pound tomatoes

3 cloves garlic, chopped

2 teaspoons chopped onions

1 teaspoon red chili powder, mild or hot, to taste

3 tablespoons peeled and thinly sliced fresh ginger

1 teaspoon salt

½ cup apple cider vinegar

12 almonds, soaked, peeled and slivered

½ cup honey

¼ teaspoon ground black cardamom

8 green cardamom pods (use only the seeds)

3 tablespoons raisins

1. Peel the tomatoes by dipping them in boiling water. The skins will shrivel up and be easy to peel off. Then cut the tomatoes into small pieces.

2. In a thick-bottomed saucepan, mix together the tomatoes, onions, ginger, garlic, chili powder, and salt and cook until the tomatoes are mushy and the sauce is thick.

3. Add the vinegar, honey, black cardamom, green cardamom seeds, raisins and almonds. Continue to cook until the mixture gets quite thick, about 15 minutes. Remove from the heat and let cool. Store in jars in the refrigerator. It will keep for a month.

Yield: about 2 cups

Note:

To peel the almonds, place them in a bowl and cover them with boiling water for a few minutes. Remove from the water. You should be able to just "pinch" the skins right off.

A Taste of India
RELISHES AND PICKLES

Sweet Chutney
(SONTH)

Easy to prepare, and very tasty.

¾ cup water	Boil the water and add the mango powder, chili powder, regular salt, garam masala, ginger, cumin and black salt. Remove from the heat. Stir in the honey and let cool.
1 teaspoon ground white cumin	
½ cup mango powder	Yield: approximately 2 cups
1 teaspoon red chili powder	
¼ teaspoon black salt (optional)	
2 teaspoons salt	
1 teaspoon garam masala	
1 teaspoon ground ginger	
½ cup honey	

Note: The black salt will smell like sulfur while cooking, but the smell disappears after the chutney cools.

Sweet Fruit Chutney
(SONTH FANCY)

A fancy version of sweet chutney—delicious!

2 cups water

2½ teaspoons red chili powder

½ cup mango powder

½ teaspoon black salt (optional)

½ cup peeled and chopped fresh ginger

½ teaspoon white cumin seeds

½ teaspoon salt, or to taste

½ cup raisins

½ teaspoons garam masala

½ cup honey

½ teaspoon beet juice (for coloring; optional)

4 bananas, peeled and sliced thin

Boil the water. Add the mango powder, black salt, chili powder, ginger, cumin, garam masala, regular salt and raisins. Remove from the heat. Stir in the honey and bananas and the beet juice. Let sit for 1 hour before serving.

Yield: about 5 cups

Note: The black salt makes a strong sulfur smell while cooking, but the smell disappears after the dish cools.

A Taste of India
RELISHES AND PICKLES

Mango Chutney
(AMB CHATNEE)

A sweet, spicy chutney for pakoras, samosas, etc.

2 green mangoes (unripe)

1 tablespoon raisins

½ cup water

2 cloves garlic

2 tablespoons peeled and thinly sliced fresh ginger

¼ cup vinegar

¼ teaspoon red chili powder

3 tablespoons chopped almonds

¾ cup honey

2 teaspoons salt

¼ teaspoon ground black cardamom

① Peel the mangoes and cut the pulp into small pieces. Place in a saucepan and cook with the water, ginger, raisins and garlic. When the mango is tender about 15–20 minutes remove from the heat.

② Add the vinegar, almonds, cardamom, chili powder, honey and salt and mix well. Cook until the mixture is thick and brown, 10–20 minutes.

③ Let cool and store in a jar in the refrigerator.

Yield: 3 cups

A Taste of India
RELISHES AND PICKLES

Spicy Sweet-Sour Mango Chutney
(NAAVRATAN CHATNEE)

Sweet and mildly salty. Great with chapatis!

2 unripe mangoes (about 3 cups)

4 bay leaves

5 teaspoons salt

½ cup water

½ cup pitted dried dates

½ cup vinegar

½–¾ cup honey

1 teaspoon black cumin seeds (if not available, use white)

½ cup vinegar

½ teaspoon ground black pepper

1 teaspoon ground cinnamon

½ teaspoon ground cloves

1 teaspoon crushed dry red chilies

½ teaspoon ground nutmeg

½ teaspoon ground cardamom

 Peel the mangoes and grate finely or chop into small pieces. Place in a thick-bottomed saucepan and add the water, bay leaves, and salt. Cover and simmer on a low heat until the mango starts getting soft, 15–20 minutes. Be sure to stir now and then to prevent sticking.

 Simmer dates in ½ cup vinegar until soft. Then strain off the vinegar, let the dates cool and slice them very thin.

1 teaspoon ground ginger

½ cup almonds, roasted and slivered

2 tablespoons pistachio nuts (shelled)

½ cup raisins

1 tablespoon fresh lime juice

3 In a thick-bottomed saucepan, mix together the honey and another ½ cup of vinegar, add the mangoes (step 1), dates (step 2), black pepper, crushed chilies, ginger, cumin, cinnamon, cloves, nutmeg and cardamom. Bring to a simmer and cook until it becomes a thick puree, stirring frequently. Add the almonds, raisins, pistachios and lime juice, and continue to simmer gently until it becomes thick. Let cool and store in a jar in the refrigerator.

Yield: approximately 4 cups

Mint Chutney
(POODEENAA IMLEE CHATNEE)

Five-minute chutney—spicy, hot and very tasty. Very good with chapatis and bland dishes. A little goes a long way!

½ cup chopped fresh mint leaves chopped

2 tablespoons honey

2 green chilies, mild or hot, to taste

2 tablespoons seedless tamarind concentrate (dissolved in 2 tablespoons of hot water), dry pomegranate seeds or lemon juice

pinch of salt

In an electric blender, blend all the ingredients. Serve fresh.

Yield: 2/3 cup

A Taste of India
RELISHES AND PICKLES

Mint and Coriander Chutney
(POODEENAA DHANEEAA KEE CHATNEE)

A delicious, spicy chutney for samosas or pakoras.

4 tablespoons fresh coriander leaves (cilantro)

2 teaspoons salt

2 tablespoons seedless tamarind concentrate

4 tablespoons fresh mint leaves

2 tablespoons honey

2 green chilies, mild or hot, to taste

8 tablespoons water

In an electric blender, blend all the ingredients. Serve fresh.

Yield: 1 cup

Lemon Chutney
(NIMBOO CHATNEE)

A pungent, sweet, sour and salty chutney that requires no cooking but does need a few days to blend.

4 lemons

1 tablespoon salt

1 black cardamom pod (use only the seeds)

¼ teaspoon red chili powder

3 whole cloves, ground

1/3 cup honey

1 Carefully wash, dry and juice the lemons. Remove the pulp and discard it. Chop the peels very fine and add them to the lemon juice. Cover and let sit, unrefrigerated, *for 3 or 4 days.*

2 Add the remaining ingredients. Store in a jar in the refrigerator. It will keep for several weeks.

Yield: 1½ cups

A Taste of India
RELISHES AND PICKLES

Turnip, Carrot and Cauliflower Pickle
(SHALGAM, GAAJAR, GOBEE ACHAAR)

A substantial, somewhat spicy side dish that complements simple rice dishes and breads. Be sure to start preparation at least two weeks before you want to serve it.

7 cups vegetables (a combination of turnips, carrots and cauliflower, chopped as indicated)

4 teaspoons crushed garlic

4 teaspoons peeled and crushed fresh ginger

⅓ cup vegetable oil

½ cup watercress

½ cup fructose (or honey and pinch of baking soda)

8 teaspoons garam masala

¼ cup cider vinegar

1 teaspoon ground mustard

1 teaspoon crushed dry red chilies

1 teaspoon salt

① Wash the vegetables thoroughly. Cut the carrots (peeled) and cauliflower into medium-sized pieces. Do not peel the turnips but cut them into medium-sized pieces.

② Heat a large pot of water to boiling, add the vegetables and leave them until the water begins to boil again. Then strain off the water and spread the vegetables out on paper towels or a clean cloth. *Let them sit for 2 hours.* Then gather them into a bowl and let them sit, unrefrigerated and uncovered, *overnight.*

③ In a thick-bottomed frying pan, heat the oil to smoking point. Remove the pan from the heat and let the oil cool, add the garlic and ginger, return to the heat and fry until they are brown. Add ½ cup of water and cook until all the water is evaporated.

④ Soak the fructose in the vinegar. Stir in the crushed chilies, garam masala, mustard, salt and garlic/ginger mix (step 1). Add the vegetables and mix well. Pack into a large jar (or jars), cover loosely and place in the sun. Stir it well at least once a day. *Fifteen days after bottling*, the pickles are ready to eat. Then store in jars and refrigerate.

Yield: approximately 6 cups

A Taste of India
RELISHES AND PICKLES

Stuffed Red Pepper Pickle
(MIRCHEE KAA ACHAAR)

A strong-bodied, spicy, moderately hot condiment. You will need to start preparation at least two weeks before you want to serve it.

1 cup fresh red chilies, large size (or small yellow chilies)

1 cup mustard oil

4 teaspoons ground fenugreek powder

7-8 teaspoons salt

9 teaspoons garam masala

3 teaspoons mango powder

2-3 teaspoons red chili powder

2 teaspoons ground white cumin

8 teaspoons fennel seed powder

1 teaspoon ground mace

juice of 1 or 2 lemons

1. Wash and dry the fresh red chilies. Cut lengthwise, scrape out the seeds and cut off the stems.

2. Heat the oil until very hot, then remove the pan from the heat and let cool.

3. In a bowl, mix together all the spices. Pour ½ cup of cooled oil over the spices and mix well. Stuff this mixture into the fresh red chilies.

4. Put the chilies in a jar, then pour in the rest of the oil and the lemon juice. *Let sit, unrefrigerated, covered loosely for 15 days.* Stir it occasionally. Then store in a jar in the refrigerator.

Yield: 1½ cups

BEVERAGES

India's beverages tend to be fairly simple: a fruit punch, warm sweetened milk or tea. They are either served alone or with snacks. Meals are accompanied by cool, pure water.

Lassi, a blended yogurt drink, is a wonderful mid-afternoon pick-me-up. Lassi comes in three varieties: with a little salt, a little honey, or just plain, depending on your taste and mood that day.

The warm milk drinks are good sources of protein and energy. Their warmth and high-calcium content make them particularly soothing pre-bedtime drinks.

Jaljeera is a spicy beverage that acts as an appetite stimulant when served chilled before a meal, or, served warm, accompanies golgappas, the little pillow-like snack wafers, as both a filling and a dip.

Date Milk
(KHAJOOL DUDH)

This drink is especially good in the evening.

4 firm dates (not mushy) without pits ½ cup water 2 cups milk 5 almonds, sliced	In a thick-bottomed saucepan, boil the dates in the water for about 2 minutes. When the dates are soft, mash them with a fork and add the milk and almonds. Bring to a boil, then simmer for 2 more minutes and remove from the heat. Serve with dates still in (blending optional). Yield: approximately 2 cups

Milk with Ghee and Almonds
(BADAAM DUDH)

A great bedtime snack!

1 tablespoon ghee 6 almonds, sliced or slivered 2 cardamom pods (use the seeds only) 2 cups milk 1–2 teaspoons honey (to taste)	In a thick-bottomed frying pan, heat the ghee and sauté the almonds until they start to brown. Crush the cardamom seeds and add along with the milk. Boil for 1 minute. Add honey to taste. Serve with almonds and cardamom seeds still in (blending optional). Yield: about 2 cups

A Taste of India
BEVERAGES

Jaljeera
(JALJEERAA)

A spicy sip or dip. Good as an appetizer or with golgappas, this "Indian lemonade" has an exotic, spicy, salty-sweet flavor.

2 quarts water

¼ cup peeled and chopped fresh ginger

⅛ cup tamarind concentrate (seedless)

2 tablespoons honey

2 small bunches of fresh mint leaves

6 green chilies, mild or hot, to taste

½ teaspoon garam masala

2 tablespoons ground white cumin

2 teaspoons black salt (or sea salt)

juice of ½ lemon

In an electric blender, blend 1½ cups of the water (reserving the rest of the water) with all the other ingredients. When totally blended, stir into the remaining water.

Serve cool as a beverage, or hot as a dip with golgappas.

Yield: about 8½ cups

Note: Golgappas are extremely thin, hollow wafers. You can make a small hole in the side of a golgappa, fill it with jaljeera and then very, very quickly pop the whole thing into your mouth. Speed is of the essence, otherwise you end up with a handful of wet crumbs and a lapful of jaljeera. First-timers can try just dipping the golgappas in the jaljeera; the taste, in the end, is the same.

A Taste of India
BEVERAGES

Seera with Whole-Wheat Flour

Dessert in a tea cup! Good as a snack or before bed; also good for colds and flu.

1 tablespoon whole-wheat flour	**❶** Sauté flour in ghee over low heat till light brown. Add almonds, pistachios, cardamom seeds and raisins. Stir well.
1 tablespoon ghee	
5 almonds, soaked, peeled	**❷** Add water, let cook till the consistency is like thick soup, then add honey and serve hot.
2 cardamom pods (seeds only)	Yield: 1 cup
5 raisins	
5 pistachios, unsalted or salt washed off, shredded	
1¼ cups water	
1 tablespoon honey, or to taste	

A Taste of India
BEVERAGES

Seera with Chickpea Flour

A hearty, spicy drink, good for sore throats and congested noses and chests.

10 almonds, soaked and peeled

4 cardamom pods (seeds only)

¼ cup water

10 pistachios, unsalted or salt washed off

1 tablespoon chickpea flour

2 tablespoons ghee

1 cup milk

1 tablespoon honey, or to taste

1 In an electric blender, process the almonds, pistachios and cardamom seeds in the water, making a paste.

2 Sauté the chickpea flour in the ghee over low heat until light brown. Add the paste from step 1. Stir well.

3 Add milk and honey and cook for a few minutes on medium heat, stirring constantly so that the milk will not curdle. Serve hot.

Yield: about 1 cup

A Taste of India
BEVERAGES

Energy Drink
(SHARDAEE)

A sweet, spicy, milky drink—very refreshing in the summer.

50 almonds (about ¼ cup)

3 tablespoons poppy (khaskhas) seeds

1 tablespoon cantaloupe seeds

1 tablespoon watermelon seeds

5 cardamom pods (green, if possible, seeds only)

1 tablespoon sunflower seeds

10 black peppercorns

1 tablespoon pumpkin seeds

1 cup water

8-10 tablespoons honey, to taste

5 cups water

4 ice cubes (optional)

Using an electric blender, thoroughly blend all the nuts, seeds, and spices in 1 cup water until a thick paste is formed. Add honey, 5 cups water and (optional) ice cubes, blend and serve. Or, let sit in the refrigerator until cold.

Yield: 6½ cups

A Taste of India
BEVERAGES

Saffron Milk
(KESREE DUDH)

A warm, fragrant, curl-up-with-a-book morning or before-bed drink.

5 threads of saffron

2 tablespoons water

1 cup milk

5 almonds, chopped

4 green cardamom pods (use only the crushed seeds)

1 teaspoon honey, or to taste

1. Soak the saffron in 2 tablespoons of water for 5 minutes.

2. Boil the milk with the green cardamom seeds for 1 minute. Then add the saffron water and almonds. Remove from the heat. Add honey to taste and stir. Serve with almonds and cardamom seeds still in (blending optional).

Yield: about 1 cup

A Taste of India
BEVERAGES

Saffron Milk with Almonds
(KESAR DADAAM DUDH)

A filling, flavorful drink. Serve hot for colds and chest congestion, or cold for an energy lift.

1¼ cups milk

6 threads of saffron

4 cardamom pods (seeds only)

5 pistachios, unsalted or salt washed off

1 tablespoon honey, or to taste

5 almonds, soaked and peeled

2 ice cubes (optional)

1. Cook milk over medium heat with cardamom seeds and saffron threads until reduced slightly, about 5 minutes

2. Using an electric blender, blend with nuts and honey and serve hot, or add ice cubes and blend again for a cold smoothie.

Yield: 1 cup

Golden Milk

A cozy drink before bed.

1 teaspoon ghee

1 tablespoon honey, or to taste

½ teaspoon ground turmeric

1 cup milk

Heat ghee in a small saucepan. Add turmeric and stir well. Add the milk and stir again. Let cook for 1 minute over medium heat, then add honey, stir and serve.

Yield: about 1 cup

A Taste of India
BEVERAGES

Banana-Almond Protein Drink

A quick breakfast energy drink.

1 cup milk

10 pistachios, unsalted or salt washed off

1 tablespoon protein powder

4 cubes ice

½ ripe banana

1 tablespoon honey, or to taste

10 almonds, soaked and peeled

In an electric blender, combine all the ingredients together thoroughly. Serve.

Yield: 2 cups

Fruit Shake

A light, delightful shake for breakfast or as a snack.

3/4 cup milk

1 cup any seasonal fruit

4 cubes ice

1-2 tablespoons honey, to taste

2 cardamom pods (seeds only)

In an electric blender, combine all ingredients together thoroughly. Serve.

Yield: about 2 cups

A Taste of India
BEVERAGES

Mango Shake

Delicious and satisfying!

1 cup milk

2 cardamom pods (seeds only)

pulp of 1 mango

4 ice cubes

1 tablespoon honey, or to taste

1 tablespoon sandalwood syrup or 2 drops sandalwood essence (optional)

In an electric blender, combine all ingredients together thoroughly. Serve.

Yield: about 2 cups

Note: If sandalwood syrup (or sandalwood essence and honey) is substituted for honey in this recipe, the drink, taken once a day for a month, is said to help make the brain alert, help prevent headache, and assist in chronic mucus problems.

A Taste of India
BEVERAGES

Mango Drink

In consistency rather like a fruit juice, this refreshing drink is said to prevent heat stroke.

Pulp of 1 mango, diced

2 tablespoons honey, or to taste

3 cups water

Cook the mango in the water until very soft. Then place, along with honey, in an electric blender and thoroughly blend. Refrigerate until cold, then serve.

Yield: about 3 cups

Plum Drink

A light, fruity drink for summer weather. Said to help prevent heat stroke and liver problems.

5 dried plums (prunes)

2 cups water

pinch of salt

pinch of black pepper

1 tablespoon honey

2 cups ice

1. Soak plums in water.

2. In the morning, boil plums in soaking water until only half the water is left.

3. Add remaining ingredients and stir well. Let cool, then serve with ice.

Yield: about 1 cup

A Taste of India
BEVERAGES

Indian Tea
(CHAI)

After a filling meal, there's nothing like a good cup of chai. Now, thanks to decaffeinated tea bags, even the health conscious can enjoy this delicious drink.

2 or 3 cardamom pods (seeds only)	Boil cardamom seeds in water until slightly reduced, about 5 minutes. Add the tea bag, cover, remove from heat and let steep for 1 minute.
1¼ cups water	
1 black tea bag	Add honey and milk. Serve hot.
2 tablespoons milk	Yield: 1 cup
1 teaspoon honey or agave, or to taste	

A Taste of India
BEVERAGES

Ginger Tea
(ADRAK CHAA)

This tea's strong gingery taste will give you energy! It's also good for colds, flu, sore throats and menstrual cramps.

2-inch stick fresh ginger, peeled and chopped

1¼ cups water

1 black tea bag

1-inch stick cinnamon

½ cup milk

2 green cardamom pods

1 tablespoon honey, or to taste

Boil ginger, cinnamon stick, and cardamom in water until reduced slightly, about 5 minutes. Add tea bag and milk, return to a boil, add honey and stir. Strain and serve.

Yield: 1½ cups

A Taste of India
BEVERAGES

Yogi Tea*

My husband, Yogi Bhajan's, special recipe. Good for the blood, the colon, the nervous system and the bones, and for colds, flu and physical weakness. That is a great deal of benefit in a small, flavorful cup of tea!

1¼ cups water

4 green cardamom pods, cracked

1 slice fresh ginger, peeled

6 black peppercorns

3 cloves

½-inch stick cinnamon

¼ teaspoon black tea

1 tablespoon honey, or to taste

½ cup milk

1 Bring the water to a boil and add the spices. Cover and continue boiling for 10–15 minutes.

2 Remove from heat, add black tea and let steep for 1–2 minutes.

3 Add honey and milk, bring to a boil, and remove from heat. Strain and serve.

Yield: 1 cup

*Pre-measured and packaged yogi tea can be purchased in many specialty food stores.

A Taste of India
BEVERAGES

Masala Tea
(MASAALAA CHAI)

Deliciously aromatic!

1½ cups water

2 cardamom pods (seeds only)

1-inch piece of fresh ginger

1-inch stick cinnamon

1 black tea bag

1 tablespoon honey, or to taste

4 almonds, soaked and peeled

½ cup milk

5 pistachios, unsalted or salt washed off

Boil spices in water until slightly reduced, about 5 minutes. Add remaining ingredients, bring to a boil, and remove from heat. Strain, if desired, and serve hot—or refrigerate and serve cold.

Yield: about 1 cup

A Taste of India
BEVERAGES

Fennel or Oregano Tea
(AJWAN CHAI)

A strong, somewhat stimulating tea; good for the digestion and to soothe an upset stomach.

1 tablespoon fennel seeds or oregano (ajwan) seeds	Boil fennel or oregano in water until slightly reduced, about 5 minutes. Add milk and tea bag and return to a boil. Add honey, mix well, strain and serve.
1¼ cups water	Yield: 2 cups
1 cup milk	
1 black tea bag	
1-2 tablespoons honey, or to taste	

Hot or Cold Lemonade

Served cold, this is a refreshing drink for summer days. Served hot, it soothes sore throats.

2 tablespoons honey	Combine honey and warm water, mixing well till honey dissolves. Add lemon juice and remaining water, cold or hot as desired. Optional: blend with ice cubes in blender.
juice of 1 lemon	
¼ cup warm water	Yield: 1 cup
about 3/4 cup water (hot or cold)	
2 cubes ice (optional)	

A Taste of India
BEVERAGES

❦
Cold, Salted Lemonade

Refreshingly different as a summer drink. In India, it is taken to prevent heat stroke.

3/4 cup water	In an electric blender, thoroughly combine all ingredients. Serve.
a pinch or two of salt	
4 ice cubes	Yield: about 1 cup
a pinch or two of black pepper	
juice of 1 lemon	

❦
Lassi

This cold yogurt shake is good for breakfast, snack or anytime.

2 cups yogurt	In an electric blender, blend the yogurt and water with a few ice cubes until bubbles form on top. Add 4 drops of rose water, lemon juice or nutmeg and either honey or salt to taste, or leave plain, and blend again. Serve very cold.
2 cups ice	
2 cups water	
4 drops rose water	Yield: 1 quart
pinch salt (optional) or 1 tablespoon honey or to taste	
juice of ½ lemon or ¼ teaspoon ground nutmeg	

A Heavenly Dessert

Baba Sheik Farid, the great fifteenth-century Muslim saint, received his early spiritual instruction from his mother. When he was but a young boy, she devised a plan to encourage him to meditate.

She told her son, "Sit quietly with your eyes closed and meditate on God. If you sit really still and concentrate very deeply, God will send down an angel to give you a reward."

While her son was meditating, she slipped into his room and hid a delicious sweet under his prayer rug. When he finished his meditation and found the treat, he ran to his mother crying, "It's true. It's true. An angel did bring me a reward!"

Farid's mother kept up this same practice every day. Years passed. One day, she became distracted by her chores and suddenly realized she had forgotten to place Farid's sweet under his prayer rug. She hurried to his room and found his body sitting straight and tall, but almost lifelessly still. Farid had gone into a deep state of meditation. Frightened as any mother would be, she called to him, "Farid, Farid, are you all right?"

The boy opened his eyes. "Don't worry, Mother. I'm fine. You needn't bring me sweets today. They were very helpful, but I don't need them anymore. Today I have been blessed with the true heavenly nectar."

Farid came to be known as "Ganj-i-Shakar," the treasury of sweetness. It is said that once, during a long fast, he placed some pebbles in his mouth to assuage his hunger. The pebbles turned into candies! Farid's birthplace has become a sacred shrine, and to this day, a free kitchen serves food to all who visit there.

SWEETS AND DESSERTS

Sweet foods play a very important part in the Indian way of life. Traditionally, meals are served in only two courses: the main course, with its rich array of bread, vegetables, yogurt and rice dishes (one of which may be sweet), followed by the sweet course. Spiritually, almost every religious ceremony includes a sweet as part of the rites of devotion, either offered to God in thanks or distributed to all as a symbol of God's blessings. And, of course, whenever snacks are served, both sweet and savory delights may be included.

Sweets are made at home, but often, with no loss of face, an Indian cook will buy them from a professional sweet-maker (*halwai*) at the sweetshop (*mithaiwala*). Unfortunately, mithaiwalas are few and far between in the West; therefore, I have included a wide variety of recipes in this chapter so, with a little extra time and effort, you can enjoy this irresistible aspect of Indian cuisine.

Sweets can be classified in two categories: "Dry" sweets are candy-like and can be eaten with the fingers. They keep well for a long time (if hidden). "Wet" sweets are slightly moist or are served in a syrup. I have also included some cake recipes that are more Western in flavor. While not strictly traditional, they are among my favorites.

A Taste of India
SWEETS AND DESSERTS

Cream Balls and Noodles in Syrup

Cheese Balls in Sweet Sauce
(RAASGULAA)

1 ½ cups chenna

1 tablespoon farina

1 cup honey

1 cup water

Place the chenna in a bowl, add the farina and mix together until it forms a smooth dough. Form into a dozen or so small balls, each about the size of a walnut.

In a large saucepan, bring the honey and water to a boil to form a syrup. Place the balls in the boiling syrup. Cook until cracks appear in the balls. Remove from the syrup and let cool before serving.

Yield: 1 dozen balls

A Taste of India
SWEETS AND DESSERTS

Cheese Disks in Pistachio Cream Sauce
(RAS MALAAI)

For the disks:

1 ½ cups chenna

1 tablespoon farina

1 cup honey

1 cup water

For the cream sauce:

1 pint half-and-half

2 drops rose water (optional)

For the topping:

1 teaspoon chopped pistachio nuts

1 teaspoon slivered almonds

1 Prepare the chenna and honey syrup as for the previous recipe but flatten the balls into thick disks. Cook in honey syrup until cracks appear, then remove from the syrup, pressing them gently to remove the excess syrup. Set aside.

2 In a thick-bottomed saucepan, cook the half-and-half over medium heat, *stirring constantly,* until it thickens. Remove from the heat, stir in rose water (optional) and soak the cheese disks in this cream for 15 minutes.

3 To serve: place the cheese disks in a bowl. Pour the cream sauce over them and sprinkle with pistachios and almonds. Chill before serving.

Yield: 1 dozen disks and 1/3 cup cream sauce.

A Taste of India

SWEETS AND DESSERTS

Sweet Cream Balls

(KHOAA LADDOO)

6 cups milk

2 tablespoons honey

½ teaspoon lemon juice

¼ teaspoon kewra essence

2 teaspoons ghee

20 pistachios, chopped fine

1 silver leaf for decoration

20 almonds, slivered

① In a large thick-bottomed saucepan, bring the milk to a boil, then reduce the heat and continue to cook, *stirring all the time*, until thickened into khoa. Add a few drops of lemon juice and stir, repeating this several times, so the milk becomes grainy in texture but not watery. Cook for 5 more minutes. Add the ghee and keep *stirring all the time* until thickening into khoa. Then add a few drops of lemon juice. Cook for 5 more minutes. Add 1 teaspoon of ghee and keep stirring until the ghee starts to separate out. Remove from the heat.

② Stir in the honey and let the mixture cool. Add the kewra essence and stir. Then roll the mixture into a dozen or so small balls, each about the size of a walnut. Arrange on a platter, sprinkle with pistachios and almonds and decorate with silver leaf.

Yield: 12–14 balls

A Taste of India
SWEETS AND DESSERTS

Gulab Jaman
(GULAAB JAAMAN)

These honey-drenched sweet balls are an Indian favorite.

For the balls:

5 teaspoons unbleached white flour

2–6 teaspoons yogurt, or enough to make a soft dough

½ teaspoon baking soda

3 teaspoons melted ghee

2 cups vegetable oil or ghee for deep-frying

1½ cups non-instant powdered milk

For the syrup:

1¼ cups honey

pinch of salt

1 cup water

Garnish:

¼ teaspoon kewra essence, or to taste (optional)

To make the balls:

 Sift together the flour and baking soda. Work the melted ghee into this mixture with your fingertips. Add the powdered milk and enough yogurt to form a very soft dough. Roll it into a dozen or so small balls each about the size of a walnut.

 In a thick-bottomed saucepan, heat the vegetable oil or ghee. Gently immerse the balls in the hot oil and deep-fry over low heat until brown. Remove with a slotted spoon, letting the excess oil drip back into the pan. Set aside.

To make the syrup:

Cook the honey, water and salt together in a saucepan until the honey is completely dissolved. Let cool.

To serve:

Add the deep-fried balls to the cooled syrup and let them sit in the syrup until they have soaked it all up, approximately 1 hour. Arrange balls on a platter and, if desired, sprinkle with kewra essence.

Yield: 1 dozen balls

A Taste of India
SWEETS AND DESSERTS

Gulab Jaman—American Style
(GULAAB JAAMAN)

Here is an easy-to-make variation on the previous recipe.

For the balls:

1 cup buttermilk pancake mix

1 cup lukewarm milk, or enough to form a smooth dough

2 cups non-instant milk powder

2 cups vegetable oil or ghee for deep-frying

4 teaspoons vegetable oil

For the syrup:

1½ cups honey

1½ cups water

To make the balls:

Sift together the buttermilk pancake mix, milk powder and baking soda. Mix in 4 teaspoons of vegetable oil. Add enough milk to form a smooth dough. Oil your hands to prevent sticking and roll the dough into small balls each about the size of a walnut.

In a thick-bottomed saucepan or wok, heat the 2 cups of vegetable oil or ghee over low heat. (If the oil is too hot, the balls will not cook at the center.) Immerse the balls in the hot oil and deep-fry until brown. Remove from the oil with a slotted spoon, letting the excess oil drip back into the pan. Drain further on paper towels.

To make the syrup:

In a saucepan, bring the honey and the water to a boil and boil for 2 minutes. Let cool.

To serve:

Add the deep-fried balls to the cooled syrup and let them soak in the syrup for at least 5 minutes. Serve warm or chilled. (These balls will keep for several weeks in the refrigerator.)

Yield: approximately 25 balls

A Taste of India
SWEETS AND DESSERTS

Honey Bits

Very sweet and tasty.

For the pastry:

1 cup khoa or unsweetened evaporated milk

1 cup unbleached white flour, or enough to form a wet dough

¼ cup panir

½ teaspoon baking soda

2 cups vegetable oil or ghee for deep-frying

½ teaspoon water

3 tablespoons farina (plain Cream of Wheat)

For the syrup:

2 cups honey

2 cups water

For decoration:

½ cup shredded coconut

To make the pastry:

 Mix the khoa and panir together well. Dilute the baking soda in ½ teaspoon water and stir in. Add the farina and enough flour to from a wet dough. Roll into thick cylinders about 2 inches long and ½ inch wide.

 In a thick-bottomed saucepan, heat the vegetable oil or ghee. Reduce the heat, immerse 6-8 pastries at a time in the hot oil and deep-fry until light brown about 3 minutes. Remove with a slotted spoon, letting the excess oil drip back into the pan. Drain further on paper towels.

To make the syrup:

In a saucepan, bring the honey and the water to a boil and boil for 2 minutes. Remove from the heat.

To serve:

Place the pastry in the hot syrup and *soak for 3 or 4 hours.* Then remove from the syrup and cut into 1-inch-thick pieces. Sprinkle with shredded coconut.

Yield: about 4 dozen pastries

Sweet Noodles
(FALOODAA)

For the noodles*:

¾ cup arrowroot flour

enough cold water to cover the noodles

3 cups water

3 cups ice in 3 cups water

*or use 1½ cups cooked thin vermicelli

For the syrup:

1 cup honey

1/8 teaspoon kewra essence (optional)

1 cup water

To make the noodles:

In a thick-bottomed saucepan, mix the arrowroot flour into the 3 cups of water very thoroughly. Cook over low heat, stirring continuously, until it starts to thicken and pull away from the sides of the pot. Place this mixture in a pasta machine and press it through the spaghetti cutter, out into a basin of ice water (3 cups ice and 3 cups water). Remove the noodles from the water and place in a deep dish. Cover with cold water.

To make the syrup:

Mix the honey and water together in a saucepan and bring to a boil. Cook until it forms a sticky syrup, about 3–5 minutes. Let cool, then stir in kewra essence (optional).

To serve:

Remove the noodles from the water. Drain well and serve with syrup poured over them.

Yield: 1½ cups

A Taste of India
SWEETS AND DESSERTS

Fragrant Sweet Noodles
(PARSEE DAA SAAVEEAAN)

Very rich and delicious as a side dish.

½–⅔ cup vegetable oil or ghee

1½ cups noodles (see recipe page 232) or use thin vermicelli

¼ cup almonds, soaked and peeled

½ cup honey

¼ cup raisins

¼ teaspoon ground nutmeg

6-8 green cardamom pods (use only the seeds, crushed)

① In a large thick-bottomed frying pan, heat the vegetable oil or ghee and sauté the almonds and raisins until the almonds are a deep brown. Remove from the ghee and set aside.

② Add the noodles to the pan and fry them until light brown. Add the water and honey and stir gently. Cook over medium heat until all the water is absorbed. Add the nutmeg, crushed cardamom seeds and the almonds and raisins. Stir well and cook over low heat for a few minutes. Can be served hot or cold.

Yield: 1½ cups

A Taste of India

SWEETS AND DESSERTS

Ice Cream and Syrup

Indian Ice Cream
(KULFEE)

2 cups milk

⅔ cup khoa or unsweetened evaporated milk

4 cardamom pods (green if possible; use only the crushed seeds)

5 teaspoons unbleached white flour

½ cup milk

⅓ cup honey

2 tablespoons slivered almonds, soaked and peeled

1 tablespoon chopped pistachios, unsalted or salt washed off, chopped

¼ teaspoon kewra essence

1 In a thick-bottomed saucepan, bring the 2 cups of milk and green cardamom seeds to a boil. Add the khoa or unsweetened evaporated milk and cook for 15 minutes, *stirring continuously*.

2 In a bowl, mix the flour and ½ cup of milk together to form a paste. Add this to the boiling milk, stirring it in thoroughly. Continue to cook and stir until the mixture thickens.

3 Pour mixture into two ice-cube trays and freeze. Serve alone or with sweet noodles (see recipe page 232).

Yield: 3 cups

A Taste of India
SWEETS AND DESSERTS

Mango Sherbet

A fruity treat, nice over ice cream or in making mango shakes or mango lassis.

4 ripe mangoes or 1 cup mango juice

¾ cup honey

1½ teaspoons lemon juice

1½ cups water

1. Extract the juice from the mangoes or use one cup of mango juice.

2. Mix together the mango juice, water, honey and lemon juice. Refrigerate and served chilled.

Yield: 3¼ cups

A Taste of India
SWEETS AND DESSERTS

Puddings

Cheese Pudding
(PANEER HALWAA)

A decorative, tasty treat.

⅔ cup honey

⅔ cup water

2 ½ cups panir

3 tablespoons cornstarch

¼ cup water

2 quarts milk

½ teaspoon kewra essence

2 teaspoons chopped pistachios, unsalted or salt washed off

1 In a thick-bottomed saucepan, cook the honey and water over very low heat, being careful not to scorch, until it becomes a thick syrup (it should hang like a thread from a spoon). Grate the panir and stir it into this syrup. Continue to cook for 2 minutes, then remove from the heat.

2 In a thick-bottomed saucepan, bring 2 quarts of milk to a boil. Mix the cornstarch with ¼ cup of water and add this to the boiling milk, stirring until it thickens slightly. Add the cooked panir in syrup, stir well and cook for 2 minutes. Remove from the heat and mix in the kewra essence.

A Taste of India
SWEETS AND DESSERTS

3 green cardamom pods (use only the seeds)

1 or 2 cherries, pitted and chopped

2 teaspoons chopped almonds, soaked and peeled

silver leaf for decoration

2 teaspoons chopped cashews

③ Transfer the pudding to a serving dish or individual dessert cups. Sprinkle with pistachios, almonds, cashews, green cardamom seeds and cherry pieces. Decorate with silver leaf. Refrigerate until serving.

Yield: 2 quarts

Note: The consistency of this pudding is a thick liquid, not gelled as with many American puddings.

A Taste of India
SWEETS AND DESSERTS

Royal Pudding
(SHAAHEE HALWAA)

In many Indian villages, there is a ceremony once a year to honor all of the young girls—from infants up to 12 years old—and to pray that they may have noble and prosperous lives. The adults of the community give them money and wash their feet, and everyone has a big plate of Royal Pudding, served piping hot!

2 cups milk

2 tablespoons honey

⅔ cup ghee

5 green cardamom pods (use only the seeds)

½ cup farina (plain Cream of Wheat)

2 tablespoons unbleached white flour

3 tablespoons khoa or unsweetened evaporated milk

15 almonds, soaked, peeled and chopped fine

½ cup raisins

½ teaspoon vanilla extract

15 pistachio nuts, unsalted or salt washed off

whipped cream (optional)

 In a thick-bottomed saucepan, bring the milk to a boil and add the honey, stirring until the honey dissolves. Remove from the heat and set aside.

 In a large thick-bottomed frying pan, heat the ghee and fry the farina, flour and green cardamom seeds until light brown. Add the boiled milk and khoa or evaporated milk, *stirring continuously* until the mixture is thick, about 5 minutes. Then mix in the almonds, pistachios and raisins and continue cooking and stirring until the ghee starts to separate out, about 2 minutes. Then remove from the heat and mix in vanilla extract. Serve hot with a dollop of whipped cream (optional).

Yield: 2 cups

A Taste of India
SWEETS AND DESSERTS

Special Occasion Pudding
(RAAJ BHOG HALWAA)

A sweet, soft cereal dessert—very rich.

⅔ cup honey

2 cups water

1 cup ghee

1 tablespoon pistachio nuts, unsalted or salt washed off

⅔ cup farina (plain Cream of Wheat)

3 black cardamom pods (use only the seeds)

1 tablespoon chopped almonds, soaked and peeled

2 tablespoons garbanzo flour

⅔ cup khoa or unsweetened evaporated milk

2 tablespoons hot ghee

① In a thick-bottomed saucepan, bring the honey and water to a boil, cooking until the honey is dissolved.

② In a thick-bottomed frying pan, heat the ghee and fry the farina and cardamom seeds. When slightly brown, stir in the garbanzo flour and continue cooking over low heat, *stirring continuously*, until golden brown about 3 minutes. Add the honey syrup, stir well, and add the khoa or evaporated milk, pistachios and almonds. Keep cooking and stirring until all the water is absorbed and the ghee starts to separate out, about 3 minutes. Remove from the heat.

③ Just before serving, pour 2 tablespoons of hot ghee over the pudding. Serve warm!

Yield: 3 cups

A Taste of India
SWEETS AND DESSERTS

Carrot Pudding
(GAAJAR KAA HALWAA)

1 cup half-and-half

4 medium carrots, washed, peeled and grated

1⅛ cups khoa or unsweetened evaporated milk

2 cups honey

12 pistachio nuts, unsalted or salt washed off, chopped

12 raisins

12 almonds, soaked, peeled and slivered

1 cup sweet butter

1 In a thick-bottomed saucepan, bring the half-and-half to a boil. Add the grated carrots. Cook, *stirring continuously*, until the carrots have absorbed all the milk, about 10–15 minutes.

2 Add the khoa or evaporated milk and continue to cook until most of the moisture evaporates and the mixture has a stiff consistency, about 10 minutes.

3 Stir in the honey, raisins, almonds, pistachios and sweet butter. Fry until a rich brown in color. Serve hot or cold.

Yield: approximately 3½ cups

A Taste of India
SWEETS AND DESSERTS

Farina Pudding
(SOOJEE KEE KHEER)

Nice for breakfast or for dessert.

4 cups milk

2 tablespoons sweet butter

1 cup farina (plain Cream of Wheat)

½ teaspoon ground cardamom (optional)

¾ cup honey

½ teaspoon salt

1 tablespoon chopped pistachios, unsalted or salt washed off

1 tablespoon slivered almonds soaked and peeled

1. In a large thick-bottomed saucepan, bring the milk to a boil.

2. In a thick-bottomed frying pan, heat the butter and fry the farina until slightly brown.

3. Sprinkle fried farina and ground cardamom (optional) over the boiling milk and simmer until the mixture becomes very thick and the farina grains are soft, about 5–10 minutes. Stir in the honey and salt.

Pour into a serving dish and decorate with pistachios and almonds.

Yield: 4 cups

A Taste of India
SWEETS AND DESSERTS

Fragrant Farina Pudding
(SOOJEE KAA HALWAA)

A very sweet treat.

¼ cup honey

1½ cups water

½ cup ghee

½ cup farina (plain Cream of Wheat)

¼ cup raisins, rinsed

½ teaspoon rose water

8 pistachio nuts, unsalted or salt washed off, chopped

2 green cardamom pods (use only the seeds)

a few raisins for garnish

8 almonds, soaked, peeled and sliced

1. In a saucepan, boil the honey and water for 5 minutes.

2. In a large thick-bottomed frying pan, heat the ghee and, *stirring continuously,* fry the farina over low heat until light brown about 2 minutes. Add the honey syrup and the raisins. Continue cooking and stirring until the liquid is absorbed and the ghee starts to separate out, about 2 minutes. Remove from the heat and stir in the rose water.

3. Pour the mixture into a serving dish. Decorate with crushed cardamom seeds, almonds, pistachios and a few more raisins.

Yield: 1–1½ cups

A Taste of India
SWEETS AND DESSERTS

Cookies and Cakes

Royal Toast
(SHAAHEE TUKAREE)

A rich dessert—serve with a light meal, or serve with fruit for breakfast.

8 thick slices of bread

2 cups vegetable oil or ghee for deep-frying

2 cups milk

8 green cardamom pods (use only the seeds)

¾ cup honey

⅔ cup khoa or unsweetened evaporated milk

¼ teaspoon kewra essence

1 tablespoon sliced almonds, Soaked and peeled

1 teaspoon chopped pistachios, unsalted or salt washed off

4 cherries, pitted and chopped

6 silver leaves

① Cut the crusts from the bread and slice diagonally in half. In a thick-bottomed saucepan, heat the oil or ghee. Fry the bread slices until golden brown. Remove with a slotted spoon, letting the excess oil drip back into the pan. Drain further on paper towels.

② In a thick-bottomed saucepan, bring the milk to a boil and then turn off the heat. Mix in the honey and green cardamom seeds until the honey dissolves. Soak the deep-fried bread in this syrup for 1 minute. Remove bread from the milk mixture and set aside.

③ In a thick-bottomed saucepan, stir the khoa or evaporated milk into the milk mixture created early and cook over low heat, *stirring continuously,* until it thickens a little about 2 minutes. Remove from heat and add kewra essence. Soak the bread in this mixture for 2 or 3 minutes, turning each piece over a few times. Remove with a flat spoon or spatula and arrange on a plate.

④ Decorate with sliced almonds, pistachios, cherries and silver leaf. Let cool before serving.

Yield: 16 half-slices

A Taste of India
SWEETS AND DESSERTS

Nutty Cookies
(NAN KATAAEE)

½ cup honey

1 teaspoon yogurt

½ cup ghee or melted sweet butter

1¾ cups unbleached white flour

½ teaspoon baking soda

½ teaspoon baking powder

2 black cardamom pods (seeds only, crushed)

40 pistachio nuts, unsalted or salt washed off, chopped

1 In a bowl, mix together the honey and ghee or melted sweet butter. (This mixture should be cool.) Add the yogurt and stir well.

2 In another bowl, sift together the flour, baking soda and baking powder. Add the dry ingredients to the honey/ghee mixture, stirring to form a thick paste. Form this into small balls, each about the size of a walnut. Roll in crushed cardamom seeds and chopped pistachios.

3 Heat the oven to 300 degrees. Place the balls on an oiled cookie sheet 1 inch apart and bake until brown. Remove from the oven and cool on a wire rack.

Yield: 2 dozen cookies

A Taste of India
SWEETS AND DESSERTS

Coconut Pastries
(NARYAAL "BISCUIT")

1 tablespoon sweet butter

1 tablespoon honey

1 tablespoon ghee

3 teaspoons milk

1 tablespoon coconut shredded

4½ tablespoons unbleached flour, sifted

¼ cup flour for dusting pastry board

½ teaspoon baking powder

1 In a bowl, beat together the butter, ghee and honey. Stir in the milk, flour, baking powder and shredded coconut. Mix thoroughly to form a dough.

2 On a lightly floured pastry board or other flat surface, roll the dough out to ½-inch thickness. Cut with a cookie cutter. Heat the oven to 350 degrees. Place the cookies on the cookie sheet and bake for 10 minutes or until golden brown. Cool on a wire rack.

Yield: 12 one-inch-square cookies

A Taste of India
SWEETS AND DESSERTS

Fruit Cake

1½ cups khoa or unsweetened evaporated milk

½ teaspoon lemon extract

½ teaspoon vanilla extract

1 cup water

3 tablespoons melted sweet butter or ghee

2 cups unbleached white flour

¼ teaspoon ground ginger

¾ cup fructose or raw sugar

pinch of salt

3 teaspoons baking powder

¾ cup assorted dried fruit, chopped

¾ teaspoon baking soda

¼ teaspoon ground cinnamon

1 In a bowl, mix together the khoa or evaporated milk, water, melted butter or ghee, vanilla and lemon extract.

2 In another bowl, sift together the flour, fructose or raw sugar, baking powder, baking soda, cinnamon, ginger and salt.

3 Add the dry ingredients to the liquid, mixing thoroughly. Next, add the dried fruits and mix again.

4 Heat the oven to 350 degrees. Oil a bread pan and pour in the batter. Bake for 30–40 minutes.

Yield: 1 loaf

A Taste of India
SWEETS AND DESSERTS

Candy

Coconut Fudge
(NARYAAL BARFEE)

2¼ cups khoa or unsweetened evaporated milk

2 tablespoons water

1½ cups fructose or 1½ cups honey and a scant pinch of baking soda

2 teaspoons water (optional)

a little beet juice for coloring

3 silver leaves for decoration

½ cup shredded coconut

1 In a thick-bottomed frying pan, cook the khoa or evaporated milk and water over low heat, *stirring continuously*. Add the fructose or honey (and baking soda) and continue cooking and stirring until the mixture will not stick to your spoon. Remove from the heat and let it cool. Then stir in the coconut. If the mixture is too thick, stir in 2 teaspoons of water.

2 Separate the mixture into two parts. In one part, mix in enough beet juice to turn it pink. Sprinkle some water on a platter and spread the white portion out on it evenly. Then spread the pink portion evenly over that. Decorate with silver leaf. Cool in the refrigerator until set. Cut into small pieces before serving.

Yield: one 8 × 10-inch sheet of fudge

Note: If honey is substituted for fructose in this recipe, the consistency will be that of soft, somewhat sticky fudge. Beat persistently during cooking to minimize this effect.

A Taste of India
SWEETS AND DESSERTS

Pineapple Cake

For the cake:

2 tablespoons butter at room temperature

¼ teaspoon pineapple extract

¼ cup milk

3 tablespoons sweetened condensed milk

½ cup honey

1¼ cups white unbleached flour

1 teaspoon baking powder

¼ teaspoon baking soda

1 teaspoon vegetable oil or ghee to oil pan

1 tablespoon flour to dust pan

Preheat oven to 300 degrees.

To make the cake:

① In a bowl, beat together the butter, sweetened condensed milk, pineapple extract, milk and honey.

② In another bowl, sift together the flour, baking powder and baking soda. Add the dry ingredients to the liquid, stirring thoroughly.

③ Oil a 9 × 12-inch baking pan with melted ghee or vegetable oil and dust lightly with flour. Pour the cake batter into the pan and bake until a toothpick inserted into the cake comes out clean, about 30–35 minutes. Remove from the oven and cool on a wire rack.

④ Remove the cake from the pan, wrap in a cloth, and store in an airtight container for at least 4 hours.

A Taste of India
SWEETS AND DESSERTS

For the decoration:

½ cup honey

¼ teaspoon pineapple extract

¼ cup lowfat milk

¼ cup canned pineapple juice

3 slices canned pineapple, chopped

½ cup chopped walnuts

a few cherries, pitted and chopped

To decorate:

1. Beat together honey and powdered milk, and then add pineapple extract and pineapple juice until slightly thick. (This icing soaks through the cake, giving it a moist, sweet taste. For a drier cake, heat the icing till it thickens.)

2. Cut the cake in half so that you have two 9 × 6-inch pieces. Spread each layer with the pineapple icing and sprinkle with chopped pineapple bits. Place one layer on top of the other. Garnish with cherries and walnuts.

Yield: One 9 × 6 × 2-inch cake

A Taste of India
SWEETS AND DESSERTS

Quick Pistachio-Almond Fudge
(PISTAA-BADAAM BARFEE)

Quick and very rich.

4½ cups sweetened condensed milk

1 tablespoon sweet butter

20 pistachios, unsalted or salt washed off

10 almonds, soaked, peeled and slivered

2 silver leaves

1 In a thick-bottomed frying pan, cook the condensed milk on a low heat, *stirring continuously* with a wire whisk and scraping the bottom frequently to prevent burning, until light brown in color and very thick, about 15 minutes.

2 Butter a cookie sheet with the sweet butter. Pour cooked condensed milk onto the sheet (it will spread out somewhat). Sprinkle with almonds and pistachios. Let cool and set (you may wish to refrigerate for extra firmness), then decorate with silver leaf. Cut this very sweet confection into very small pieces before serving.

Yield: one 11 × 15-inch sheet of (thin) fudge

A Taste of India
SWEETS AND DESSERTS

Almond Fudge
(BADAAM BARFEE)

3 tablespoons almonds, soaked and peeled

3 tablespoons water

1 tablespoon vegetable oil or ghee for frying

3 tablespoons fructose or 3 tablespoons honey and a scant pinch of baking soda

2½ tablespoons khoa or evaporated milk unsweetened

1–2 drops kewra essence

1 teaspoon vegetable oil to oil plate

silver leaf for decoration

① Grind the almonds to the consistency of meal, either in an electric blender or coffee mill, or use almond powder.

② In a small saucepan, heat the fructose or honey (and baking soda) with the water and cook over low heat, stirring continuously being careful not to scorch, until a sticky syrup is formed, about 3–5 minutes.

③ In a thick-bottomed frying pan, heat the oil or ghee and fry the khoa or evaporated milk over low heat, *stirring continuously,* until light brown and oil or ghee is just starting to separate out, about 4 minutes. Remove pan from heat, add almonds, syrup and kewra essence and mix well.

④ Spread this mixture out on an oiled plate and *let set for 3 or 4 hours* in refrigerator. Before serving, decorate with silver leaf and cut into small pieces.

Yield: 9 small pieces

A Taste of India
SWEETS AND DESSERTS

❦

Cream Mixed Fruit Bark
(PISTAA BARFEE)

A chewy, nutty confection. The cardamom adds a touch of the exotic.

3 cups khoa or unsweetened evaporated milk

½ cup fructose or ½ cup honey and a pinch of baking soda

2 tablespoons chopped almonds, soaked and peeled

6 green cardamom pods (use only the seeds)

1 teaspoon vegetable oil to oil cookie sheet

2 tablespoons chopped pistachios, unsalted or salt washed off

3 silver leaves

1 In a thick-bottomed saucepan, mix together the khoa or evaporated milk and fructose or honey (and baking soda) and cook over low heat until the sweetener is dissolved. Remove from the heat and *beat well* with a spoon, then return to low heat and continue to cook, *stirring continuously*. When the mixture no longer feels sticky to your fingertip, add the almonds, pistachios and cardamom seeds and stir.

2 Spread the mixture out evenly on an oiled cookie sheet. Let sit 3 or 4 hours to set. Decorate with silver leaf and cut into small pieces before serving.

Yield: one 4 × 8-inch sheet of (thin) candy

A Taste of India
SWEETS AND DESSERTS

Coconut Squares
(NARYAAL TIKKEE)

A fast, simple treat.

3 slices whole-wheat bread

2 tablespoons honey

½ cup unsweetened evaporated milk

¼ teaspoon salt

¼ cup dry, grated coconut

1. Cut the crusts from the bread. Cut each slice of bread into quarters.

2. Mix together the evaporated milk, honey and salt. Dip each piece of bread into this mixture. Sprinkle the top with grated coconut.

3. Heat the oven to 350 degrees. Place the bread on a wire rack, coconut side up, and bake until golden brown, about 15 minutes. Serve hot.

Yield: 12 squares

The Guru's Lesson

Guru Gobind Singh taught that each person should think of his own home as a free kitchen. Whatever food was in his cupboard did not truly "belong" to him; it was merely in his custody to be used to feed whoever might be in need.

The Guru decided to test his disciples to see how well they practiced hospitality as he taught it. Disguised as a lowly beggar, he went to their homes late in the evenings and humbly requested some food. When his survey was complete, he gathered his congregation together and made his report:

"I'm glad to say that in none of the homes I visited was the 'lowly beggar' turned away empty handed. Even the least gracious among you asked him to wait at the door while you fetched some leftover breads or sweets for him to take on his way.

"Those who were more generous invited the man to come in. They explained that they had no food ready, but bade him wait while they fixed something.

"But the true spirit of the free kitchen was only practiced by one man, my disciple Nand Lal. When the beggar arrived at his door, he welcomed him in the name of God and asked him to come in. Then he quickly went to the kitchen and returned carrying a sack of wheat, a sack of beans and a container of yogurt. 'Kind sir,' he said, 'all of this food is yours for God has provided it. Now please be kind enough to let me prepare it for you.'"

SPECIAL INGREDIENTS AND WHERE TO FIND THEM

Indian cooking is most enjoyable when your kitchen is well stocked with the spices and ingredients that give Indian cuisine its distinctive flavors. Here is a list of items that you are not likely to find in your local supermarket, what they are, and their Indian names.

Following the list of ingredients is a partial listing of specialty food stores throughout North America that stock a variety of Indian ingredients.

ASAFOETIDA, *hing;* old herbal texts call it "Devil's dung;" it does have a fairly "fetid" (rotten) smell, hence its name. Upon frying, in oil, it undergoes a magical transformation and takes on an onion-like flavor. Made from the juices of plants of the fennel family, it is used medicinally as an anti-spasmodic.

BASMATI (*basmaatee*) **RICE;** a special long-grained, aromatic white unpolished rice imported from India. Texmati, a North American rice, is a good substitute.

BITTER MELON, *karelaa;* a small, green, bumpy-skinned, cucumber-shaped melon.

CARDAMOM, *ilaaechee;* a highly aromatic spice, it comes in pods, seeds or ground. The pods come in two colors, *green* and *black* or dark brown. (The white pods are just green pods that have been bleached). The little black seeds are used, and the pods discarded. *Where recipes require black cardamom, green can be substituted.*

A Taste of India
SPECIAL INGREDIENTS AND WHERE TO FIND THEM

CHAPATI FLOUR, *aatta*; a finely ground whole-wheat flour similar to whole-wheat pastry flour. "Golden Temple Chapati Flour" can be ordered by phone or mail from Spice and Sweet Mahal Store, 135 Lexington Ave., New York, NY 10016, 212-683-0900.

CHICKPEA FLOUR, *besan*; also known as gram flour or garbanzo bean flour.

CINNAMON, *daalcheenee;* literally means "sweet wood"; the dried inner bark of an evergreen tree of the laurel family; it comes rolled in short sticks (quills), bark chips or ground. Stick cinnamon is available in some supermarkets.

CITRIC ACID, *nimboo kaa sar;* used to split milk into curds and whey in the making of panir; *tartaric acid or lemon juice may be substituted;* also available in powdered form.

CORIANDER, *dhaneeaa* (cilantro, Chinese parsley); very distinctive pleasant, slightly pungent taste; used as fresh leaves, seeds and ground. Available in many supermarkets.

A Taste of India
SPECIAL INGREDIENTS AND WHERE TO FIND THEM

CUMIN, *jeeraa*; a strongly aromatic and slightly nutty spice, it comes in three types—*white*, *black* or *brown*—and is used either whole or ground. *White cumin is the most commonly used and may be substituted for the less common varieties.*

DAHL, *daal*; describes all varieties of beans. Specialty shops may stock a dozen or more varieties in bulk. Be sure to clean and rinse thoroughly before using.

FARINA, wheat meal; commonly found in U.S. grocery stores in the breakfast cereal aisle under the trade name Cream of Wheat. Use the Original 10-Minute (stovetop) variety.

FENUGREEK, *kasoon methee*; small triangle-shaped seeds with a licorice-like flavor; used whole or ground. Available in many supermarkets.

GINGER, *adrak*; often referred to as a root, ginger is actually a rhizome. Use whole, dried or ground. Available in many supermarkets.

KASOON METHI. See Fenugreek.

KEWRA ESSENCE, *rooh kewra*; a highly fragrant essence of the screw pine, used in desserts; available in bottles from specialty stores as "kewra water."

LOTUS ROOT, *kanwal kakree*; the root of the lotus flower; available peeled and canned from specialty stores, may be ordered by phone or mail. A 14-ounce can is roughly equivalent to four 6-inch-long roots.

MANGO POWDER, *ambchoor*; used as a souring agent, like lemon juice; made from unripe mangoes, peeled, dried and powdered.

MUSTARD OIL, a hot, aromatic oil, used for pickles.

NUTMEG, *jaiphal*; can be obtained whole from specialty stores. Grind with mortar and pestle, electric grinder or food processor.

POMEGRANATE POWDER, *anaardaanaa*; the dried, powdered seeds of the pomegranate, also known as the Chinese apple, used as a sweet-and-sour agent.

RICE POWDER, used as a thickener. *Substitute cornstarch or whole-wheat pastry flour.*

SAFFRON, *kesar*; a yellow aromatic spice made from the stigmas of crocus flowers; also, the world's most expensive spice!

SANDALWOOD ESSENCE, an aromatic essence of the sandalwood tree, available in bottles.

A Taste of India
SPECIAL INGREDIENTS AND WHERE TO FIND THEM

SILVER LEAF, *vark;* a decorative foil that contains pure silver. It is edible and is believed to have medicinal properties.

TAMARIND, *imlee;* the sweet-and-sour fruit of a tropical tree. It comes in a paste with the seeds still in it, or in a seedless concentrate; used as a sweet-sour agent.

TARTARIC ACID, *imlee kaa sat;* a souring agent, used for splitting milk in curds and whey when making panir; citric acid or lemon juice can be substituted.

WHITE PEPPER. If unavailable, substitute the more common black variety.

WHITE POPPY SEEDS, *khaskhas.* Raw, they are odorless, tasteless and off-white; ground, they smell much like roasted sesame oil, used as a thickening agent.

Where to Purchase Ingredients

Today, there are many Indian grocery stores or International grocery stores that stock the items listed above. Search the internet for "Indian food + your city," or "Indian grocery + your city," and you will find there are options available in most major cities. However, if you do not find a location close to you, most Indian grocery stores are also happy to accept your orders by phone or mail. If you are unfamiliar with Indian ingredients, you can also request that the items you order be labeled *in English*.

INDEX

Aattaa 154

Achaar 193, 204, 205

Ajwan 49 – 53, 61 – 63, 82, 87, 94, 98, 104, 160, 205, 222

Anise 86

Asafoetida 64, 86, 87, 114, 115, 258

Ayurvedic 15

Baryani 69

Basmati 16, 41, 167, 258

Bhajia 5, 68, 75

Bhujia 6, 68, 114

Bitter Melon 5, 101, 102, 117, 258

Black Cardamom 34, 108, 196, 199, 203, 241, 246, 258

Black Cumin 56, 58, 200

Black Mustard Seeds 147

Burfi 31, 249, 252 – 254

Camritsari Chole 162

Cardamom Pods 24, 34, 85, 107 – 109, 111, 168, 169, 172, 173, 175 – 178, 182, 196, 208, 210 – 216, 218 – 221, 235, 236, 238, 240, 241, 244 – 246, 254

Cardamom Seeds 24, 34, 85, 107 – 109, 111, 168, 172, 173, 175 – 178, 182, 196, 208, 210 – 216, 218 – 221, 235, 236, 238, 240, 241, 244 – 246, 254

Chaawal 167, 168

Chai 218, 221, 222

Chapati 22, 153 – 158, 163, 259

Chapati Flour 154, 156, 158, 163, 259

Chat Masala 5, 64

Chenna 29, 30, 228, 229

Chickpeas 5, 8, 60, 74 – 77, 92, 104, 106, 108, 162, 174, 175, 181, 182, 188, 211, 259

Chutney 7, 8, 22, 41, 47, 48, 55, 66, 76, 110, 144, 162, 193 – 203

Coriander Leaves 25, 40, 42, 45, 46, 48, 54, 70, 75, 77, 83, 85, 86 – 88, 100, 106, 108, 109, 113 – 115, 118, 123, 128 – 130, 135, 138, 142, 143, 146 – 148, 183, 185, 187, 189, 190, 202

Dahl 5, 7, 8, 17, 22, 27, 56, 74, 95, 106, 137, 179, 181, 184 – 186, 190, 260

Dais 67

Fenugreek 26, 75, 77, 205, 260

Farina 9, 45, 59, 60, 228, 229, 233, 240, 241, 243, 244, 260

Garam Masala 25, 29, 34, 35, 46, 71, 75, 82, 86 – 88, 90, 92, 99, 104, 106 – 109, 113 – 119, 164, 165, 174, 183, 184, 188, 190, 197, 198, 204, 205, 209

Garbanzo Flour 5, 48, 55, 66, 766, 92, 106, 108, 241

Ghee 4, 8, 17, 25, 29, 32, 33, 40 – 48, 54 – 62, 65, 66, 68, 70 – 72, 74 – 82, 84, 87 – 90, 92, 94 – 96, 98, 100 – 102, 104, 107, 110, 112, 114 – 118, 121, 128, 133, 151, 155 – 159, 161 – 163, 165, 168 – 179, 183 – 186, 188 – 190, 208, 210, 211, 214, 230 – 233, 235, 240, 241, 244 – 248, 250, 253

Golgappas 60, 207, 209

Green Cardamom 26, 34, 84, 85, 96, 97, 107 – 111, 168, 169, 172 – 178, 181, 182, 194, 196, 213, 219, 220, 235, 236, 238, 240, 244, 245, 254

Gulab Jaman 9, 11, 21, 179, 256

Guru 9, 25, 231, 232

Halwai 227

Hindu 21, 179

Jaljeera 8, 60, 207, 209

A Taste of India
INDEX

Kabobs 4, 40, 46, 47

Kari 68

Karma 20

Katoori 22

Kewra Essence 169, 172, 178, 230, 231, 234, 236, 238, 245, 253, 260

Khaskhas 212, 261

Khoa 4, 29, 31, 172, 178, 230, 233, 236, 240, 241, 242, 245, 248, 249, 253, 254

Koftas 6, 25, 68, 104, 105, 106, 108, 112

Kundalini 1, 2, 16

Laddu 29

Lassi 8, 23, 207, 223, 227, 237

Lotus Root 6, 74, 76, 98, 104, 106, 108, 260

Mango Powder 35, 64 – 66, 82, 100, 102, 116, 117, 182, 195, 197, 198, 205, 260

Mannu 21

Matar Panir 29

Mithaiwala 227

Mung Bean 5, 7, 52, 56, 147, 164, 173, 184, 186

Mung Bean Sprouts 147

Mustard Oil 86, 205, 260

Mustard Powder 40, 42, 149

Pakora 199, 202

Panir 4, 6, 17, 29, – 31, 66, 78, 79, 96, 106, 110, 111, 114, 169, 177, 233, 238, 259, 261

Paparies 60

Pathuras 162

Phulka 157

Pilafs 22

Pilau 69

Pink Lentils 58

Pomegranate Powder 260

Pomegranate Seeds 55, 116, 117, 188, 201

Prana 2

Pranthas 7, 155, 158 – 161

Puffed Rice 146

Punjabi 5, 17, 58, 62

Pullao 69

Puris 7, 163 – 165

Raita 6, 22, 137, 138, 141, 144, 145, 168, 190

Rajasic 15

Rasmalai 29

Sabji 68

Saffron 8, 172, 213, 214, 260

Samosas 22, 25, 54, 199, 260

Sattvic Bhoj 15

Shakti 13

Shiva 13

Sikh 20, 179

Subji 22

Subzi 68

Tamarind 75 – 77, 100, 144, 201, 202, 209, 261

Tamasic 16

Texmati 16, 167, 258

Thali 22

Tofu 5, 6, 53, 78, 96, 120 – 134

Turmeric 15, 17, 66, 71, 74 – 76, 80, 86, 88 – 90, 92 – 94, 96, 98, 100, 101, 104 – 107, 110 – 113, 116 – 118, 121, 128 – 130, 184, 185, 188, 214

Urad Dahl 56, 186

White Cumin 46, 77, 82, 108, 109, 177, 197, 198, 205, 209, 260

White Pepper 40, 85, 149, 150, 261

White Poppy Seeds 84, 261

White Squash 6, 98

Yoga 2, 15, 16, 20

Yogi 2, 3, 13, 18, 21, 64, 67, 153, 220

Yogi Bhajan 2, 13, 18, 21, 220

Yogurt
4, 6 – 8, 17, 22, 25, 29, 36, 49, 50 – 53, 58, 62, 67, 86, 87, 101, 104, 105, 109, 111, 114, 115, 137 – 150, 161, 164, 168, 171, 173, 179, 186, 195, 207, 223, 226, 231, 246, 256

ABOUT THE AUTHOR

Bhai Sahiba Bibiji Inderjit Kaur Khalsa, PhD, affectionately known as Bibiji, was born in 1935 in India (now West Pakistan). As the daughter of a devoted Sikh family, she grew up steeped in the Sikh traditions of community and service. She studied at Punjab University and later completed her M.A. at the University of New Mexico and her PhD in marriage and family counseling at the University of Humanistic Studies in California.

When she was eighteen years old, she married the world-renowned yogi and religious leader, Siri Singh Sahib Bhai Sahib Dr. Harbhajan Singh Khalsa Yogiji (1929-2004), known and loved around the world as Yogi Bhajan. They raised three beautiful children, two sons and one daughter, and they have five grandchildren. Bibiji has long amazed family, friends, and her worldwide community with a capacity to create lavish, gourmet delights for hundreds of guests, seemingly effortlessly. She serves the poor and heads of states alike, with a grace and dignity that makes her guests feel they are being served like royalty. Her kindness and compassion for all have made her a truly exceptional hostess.

In addition to teaching the Art of Indian cooking, Bibiji holds the esteemed office of Bhai Sahiba or Chief Religious Minister of Sikh Dharma and she is an active family counselor and psychologist. Among millions around the globe, Bibiji is known as a revered "mother," an ambassador of good will, and harbinger of interfaith dialogue among religious and political leaders. Bibiji is the author of six books and is the recipient of countless awards for her outstanding community service, including proclamations from Governors Bruce King and Bill Richardson of New Mexico. She is a recipient of the honorific Panth Rattan or "Jewel of the Nation" from her India homeland; she founded **Create Inner Peace**, for first responders; and she is honored by the History Museum of New Mexico with photos in the main gallery; Bibiji is sought as public speaker and teacher and travels widely, residing in New Mexico with her family and Sikh community.

A Taste of India
ABOUT THE AUTHOR

Other books by Bibiji:

A Taste of India (first edition)

Stories to Win the World

Living Reality

Psyche of the Soul

Psyche of the Golden Shield

Siri Guru Granth Sahib Darshan